In *Sex Dolls, Robots and Woman Hating*, Caitlin Roper has done compendious research to show what sex dolls and robots are for, how they are developing and how men are using them. It must have been disturbing to do this work, but Roper does a great service to feminism in telling us all that we need to know about their impact on the status of women and children. She details the vicious woman hating abuse that men practise on the dolls, which provides a whole education in the way men despise women. Sex dolls and robots are better than live women, the punters say, because they can be endlessly violated and torn apart without any complaint. I did wonder who would be doing the housework! This is a crucial book for the campaign to stop the sex doll and robot industry.

> —Sheila Jeffreys, PhD, author of *Penile Imperialism: The Male Sex Right and Women's Subordination* and *Trigger Warning: My Lesbian Feminist Life*

Read *Sex Dolls, Robots and Woman Hating: The Case for Resistance* only if you are willing to face harsh realities about 21st century misogyny. I won't soon forget the disturbing practices that Caitlin Roper describes, but I also will carry with me the power of her incisive analysis and passionate call for resistance. As I read this book, my heart broke page by page, and at the same time I was bolstered by Roper's courage. I'm grateful for her willingness to study this chilling intensification of the objectification of women, which takes sexism and racism to new levels of corrosiveness. The work of Roper and Collective Shout has never been more important.

> —Robert Jensen, emeritus professor, University of Texas at Austin and author of *The End of Patriarchy: Radical Feminism for Men*

T0244361

Caitlin Roper's *Sex Dolls, Robots and Woman Hating: The Case for Resistance,* is both brilliant and chilling. Her in-depth analysis of how sex dolls and robots are tied into the misogynist commercial sex industry brings to light the degree to which woman- and girl-hating are both monetized and normalized. Roper's call for global resistance to the objectification of women and girls cannot be ignored after reading this tour de force of a book!

—Gail Dines, PhD, Professor Emerita of Sociology,
President: Culture Reframed

Caitlin Roper is an activist, writer and Campaigns Manager at Collective Shout: for a world free of sexploitation, a grassroots campaigning movement against the objectification of women and sexualisation of girls in media, advertising and popular culture. She has a Bachelor of Music Education from the University of Western Australia and a Graduate Diploma in Arts (Sociology and Anthropology) where she was awarded the Julie Manville Memorial Prize.

Caitlin is an opinion writer whose work has been published in a range of mainstream media outlets including *The Guardian*, ABC, *Huffington Post*, *Sydney Morning Herald* and *Arena* magazine. She has been featured on *The Project, Lateline, Flashpoint*, Channel 7 News, Channel 9 News and Triple J *Hack*. She contributed a commentary chapter to *Prostitution Narratives: Stories of Survival in the Sex Trade* (Spinifex Press, 2016).

Caitlin Roper is a founding member of Adopt Nordic WA which advocates for implementation of the Nordic model of prostitution legislation in Western Australia. She has been a speaker and organiser for Reclaim the Night Perth. She is a co-founder of the Feminist Academy of Technology and Ethics (the FATES).

SEX DOLLS
ROBOTS
AND WOMAN HATING

THE CASE FOR RESISTANCE

CAITLIN ROPER

We respectfully acknowledge the wisdom of Aboriginal
and Torres Strait Islander peoples and their custodianship
of the lands and waterways. Spinifex offices are situated
on Djiru and Bunurong Country.

First published by Spinifex Press, 2022

Spinifex Press Pty Ltd
PO Box 5270, North Geelong, VIC 3215, Australia
PO Box 105, Mission Beach, QLD 4852, Australia
women@spinifexpress.com.au
www.spinifexpress.com.au

Edited by Renate Klein, Pauline Hopkins and Susan Hawthorne
Cover design by Deb Snibson, MAPG
Typesetting by Helen Christie, Blue Wren Books
Typeset in Arno Pro
Printed in the USA

A catalogue record for this
book is available from the
National Library of Australia

ISBN: 9781925950601 (paperback)
ISBN: 9781925950618 (ebook)

To Melinda Liszewski, one of the most brilliant women I know. Your passion in the fight to end the sexual exploitation of women and girls inspires me every day.

Acknowledgements

I would like to express my deepest gratitude to the wonderful women at Spinifex Press. To Renate Klein and Susan Hawthorne, thank you for believing in me and in this book. I have dreamed of one day becoming a Spinifex author, and now I am.

To Renate, Susan and Pauline Hopkins, thank you for your work to make this book better. I know that given the difficult subject matter it couldn't have been easy to work so closely on it. Thank you to the rest of the Spinifex team, Maralann Damiano and Rachael McDiarmid. Thank you to Deb Snibson for the impactful cover, and to Helen Christie for the typesetting.

To the brilliant women at 'Robot club', the co-founders of the Feminist Academy of Technology and Ethics (the FATES) – Kathleen Richardson, Viviane Morrigan, Shirley MacWilliam, Charlotta Odlind, Melissa Mallows, Lydia Delicado-Moratalla and Jo Bartosch – I am in awe of you. Thank you for sharing your insights, for allowing me to fine-tune my analysis, and for your friendship.

I would like to thank the amazing team at Collective Shout. MTR, I am so grateful for the time and energy you have put into this project and for your helpful feedback. To all of you – MTR, Melinda L, Lyn, Renee and Dan – I appreciate your support so much. You keep me sane in this fight.

To my dear friends Liz and Ari, your love and encouragement throughout this process has meant so much to me. Dave, thank you for giving me the idea in the first place! Justin, words cannot express how grateful I am to you for your ongoing support, for cheering me on and taking a copy of my manuscript with you on your surf trip so you could make edits between surfs. To Jack, Isabel and Sophia, your enthusiasm means the world to me – and no, you're still not allowed to read this book!

Contents

Introduction

Whenever someone asks me what I do for work, about my research or the subject of the book I'm writing – this book – I always pause for a moment and contemplate my response. Can they handle it? Am I prepared to have this conversation? And what's the etiquette for having it at a restaurant, a party, at school pick-up, or a wedding at which I'm a guest? (Yes, this has come up at multiple weddings.) When I cautiously reveal that the topic of my study is sex robots, I am typically met with a range of fairly predictable responses. Some are taken aback, but polite. (Fair enough – they probably didn't see that coming.) Others are fascinated and want to debate the pros and cons of sex robot technology. My least favourite response is always from a man – a comment along the lines of, "If you need someone to test them out, let me know!" while I inwardly groan.

While many people might regard sex dolls and robots – and their users – as being a bit strange, or at least, not their thing, they don't necessarily see them as harmful. But the growing trade in sex dolls and robots modelled on the bodies of women and girls, marketed for men's on-demand sexual use, has serious real-world consequences for all women and girls.

Sex dolls and robots made in the female form – which they typically are – legitimise and entrench the sexual objectification of women, reinforcing women's less-than-human status and the belief that women exist for men's sexual use. The sexual objectification of women serves as the foundation for men's violence against women in all its forms. It all begins with objectification.

If women are regarded as objects, rather than human subjects, it is easy to justify their abuse and mistreatment. Take pornography for example; if men saw women as human beings like them, they could not be aroused by their sexualised abuse and degradation in pornography. Men find pleasure in the humiliation and suffering of these women because they see them as the means of their sexual gratification, as tools, things, not as *fully human*.

If we are to address the global epidemic of male violence against women, we need to challenge the objectification of women, the belief that women are objects for men's pleasure and gratification. We are at last beginning to engage in a meaningful dialogue about men's violence and the cultural factors that drive it.

But the trade in female-bodied sex dolls and robots – replica women produced for men's sexual use – is in direct opposition to the fight against male violence. Instead of challenging the view of women as sexual objects, the production of sex dolls and robots in the female form *reinforces* the objectification of women and strengthens the notion that men are entitled to sex.

If our objective is to end men's violence against women, to advance the status of women or to create a more equitable society, sex dolls and robots are taking us in the wrong direction.

Hanging from meat hooks in multiple factories around the world, pornified female-bodied sex dolls and robots represent the literal objectification of women – embodied female objects to be owned and used; replica women, 'love dolls', 'silicon wives' or 'pornbots' produced for men's sexual gratification and unlimited sexual use. They are marketed as companions, as a 'perfect girl-friend' that can be hung up and stored away after its use.

Men who own sex dolls use them as stand-ins for women and children. Some enact violence, torture and scenarios of sexual predation on their dolls. They document this in pornographic photos and videos shared to online forums, where they are met

2

with encouragement from other doll owners. Some report using dolls as practice for sexual relations with women.

Some men prefer their sex doll to their wife, even choosing their silicone doll over their family. No woman in such a relationship can keep up with her husband's sexual demands, and she will suffer humiliation and distress over her inability to compete with a 'perfect', compliant pornographic doll. At the same time, women are subjected to grooming and gaslighting from all angles, encouraging them to tolerate their partner's sex doll use, warning them not to 'kink-shame' and urging them to 'call in a sex doll as your back up'.

Sex dolls can be customised, allowing men to build their own ideal woman. They can also be modelled on actual women and girls, without their knowledge or consent. One woman only learned about the sex doll made in her likeness when the man who created it sent her a private message on Instagram to let her know just how much he enjoyed using it. Other men exchange images online of sex dolls and robots they claim to have had customised in the likeness of specific women, for the express purpose of humiliating and violating them.

Dolls are also made in the form of children, typically girls. Child sex abuse dolls can be modelled on the bodies of toddlers and babies, complete with penetrable orifices. Men can even 'adopt' child sex abuse dolls from an 'orphanage' and 'become a Daddy'. Some use their dolls, even infants, to produce child sexual abuse material which they distribute in paedophile forums, where it is enjoyed by other forum participants who make requests for future videos.

Defenders of female-bodied sex dolls and robots, who are mostly men, argue we should welcome these pornographic dolls that offer many benefits. But the question is, for whom?

According to sex industry representatives, sex robot technology is one of the biggest trends in the industry: a game-changer. News media outlets frequently report on the latest developments around sex robots.

Sex dolls and robots made in the form of women are increasingly becoming a part of mainstream popular culture. They feature in Hollywood films – often as a female love interest – TV shows, Netflix comedy specials and documentaries. Pop star Ariana Grande even pretends to be a sex robot in a recent music video.

Sex doll venues are popping up around the world, from sex doll 'experience' cafes to doll brothels. Sex dolls have been used to fill seats in restaurants and football stadiums in response to COVID-19 restrictions.

A growing number of porn sites are dedicated to sex doll-themed pornography. Female porn performers are having dolls made in their likeness. Sex dolls even have their own Instagram and OnlyFans accounts.

This was not an easy book to write. Through my research, I have been forced to confront some of the worst humanity has to offer. As I have read the words of doll owners, manufacturers, advocates, paedophiles and men's rights activists – all defending men's access to sex dolls in the form of women and girls – I have come to understand how so many men truly perceive women.

I wrote this book to expose the inherent misogyny in the trade of female-bodied sex dolls and those who profit from it.

I wrote it to expose the misogyny of the men who purchase sex dolls – men who believe a female-shaped object with penetrable orifices can function as a stand in for a woman, and who prefer porn-star breasts over consciousness in a female 'partner'.

I wrote it to expose the misogyny of the academics, advocates and paedophile apologists who use their influence to defend the production of replica women and children for men's sexual use, who portray these products as neutral and harmless, and who encourage their development. They either never paused to consider the harms to women and girls, or simply concluded men's orgasms mattered more.

But perhaps most importantly, I wrote this book to inspire readers to action. It is my hope that after reading it, individuals will be both motivated and equipped to challenge the production of sex dolls and robots – the embodiment of woman hating – and to speak out against these developments.

CHAPTER ONE

Real men and unreal women

She is seated, dressed in sheer black lingerie and knee-high stockings, her long, wavy hair falling over her face. The sounds of the crowd can be heard in the background, and men stand around waiting for their turn. A sign nearby reads, 'BLOW JOB ROBOT TRY IT'.

It is the 2019 Adult Video News expo, the annual trade show for the porn industry, held in Las Vegas. MISSDOLL SWALLOW, billed as the first oral sex robot in the world, is the feature in a live demonstration.

A man holding a dildo approaches, sweeping her hair out of her face. With her head robotically bobbing up and down, he inserts the dildo in her mouth.

"It can go faster," he tells onlookers. He turns back to the robot, and says, "Go faster."

The robot follows his instructions.

"And it can go even faster," he boasts.

The robot speeds up again, uttering the words, "Yes, master."

Photos from the event show grinning men taking their turns, testing the robot with a dildo and posing for pictures. One man, wearing a Pornhub t-shirt, poses with his head back and eyes closed feigning sexual pleasure, carefully positioning himself so it appears the robot is performing oral sex on him, and not the dildo he is holding.

Another image shows the female-bodied robot on the chair, with one man manipulating its body and another holding a dildo to its lips, and other men standing around watching. It looks eerily reminiscent of a gang-rape scenario.

The robot speaks every now and then, saying, "Come on baby, here it is" and "Sex is fun, yes master."

The men are smiling and laughing. They are having a good time with this replica woman manufactured to sexually service men like them.

Watching men bonding over replicating scenarios of violation and humiliation on this female-bodied robot, the inherent misogyny of sex dolls and robots is undeniable. She is not really a 'she', but an 'it'. Sex dolls and robots are objects, but they are not neutral – they are an expression of woman hating.

These products could only be conceived of in a society in which women are seen as less than human, as things for men's sexual use and gratification. It's no coincidence that sex dolls and robots are overwhelmingly made in the likeness of women, for men's sexual use, rather than the other way around.

Female-bodied sex dolls for men's sexual use

Sex dolls are lifelike, full-size, anatomically correct dolls with penetrable orifices, marketed for men's sexual use. They are typically gendered female and designed to resemble the surgically enhanced bodies of female 'porn stars', with exaggerated sexual features, large breasts and tiny waists. So-called sex robots typically have a silicone sex doll body that is paired with an animatronic head and equipped with artificial intelligence.

Advocates for sex dolls and robots pitch the products as potential intimate partners and companions, and argue they could be utilised by the elderly, those who are physically or mentally disabled, for individuals who struggle with anxiety or grief, for sex education, within intimate relationships, or even for violent and abusive sexual practices, including paedophilic use. What is not acknowledged, however, is the highly gendered nature of this phenomenon.

Replicating the dynamics of the global sex trade, the sex doll industry is fuelled by male demand. The vast majority of dolls are embodied female, and buyers are overwhelmingly men. According to a spokesperson from Abyss Creations, the manufacturer of world-famous RealDoll, more than 95 per cent of their customers are men (Kleeman, 2020, p. 19).

One study of members of a sex-doll-owner online forum found that doll owners were predominantly single, white, middle-aged, heterosexual men with jobs (Valverde, 2012). Doll owners purchase dolls primarily for sexual use, although some regard their dolls as companions or report feeling an emotional attachment to them.

While there are some male-bodied dolls on the market, these are not in response to any known market demand. The quality of the male dolls is also noticeably inferior, and they don't seem to be selling very well. RealDoll has 17 different bodies and 34 face options for female-bodied dolls, but only two bodies and three face options for male dolls. Male dolls are 'on the backburner' at RealDoll, with a staff member explaining, "At the end of the day, we are still a business, and if we had more people buying them, more people interested, we'd devote more time to them" (Kleeman, 2020, p. 21).

Male sex dolls appear to be merely tokenistic – RealDoll creator Matt McMullen reportedly created male-bodied sex robot Henry to "represent both genders" and shut down claims the company was objectifying women (Davis, 2018).

Often, even where male-bodied sex dolls exist, they are still marketed to men. Lumidolls, a Spanish company that opened the world's first sex doll brothel, have two male dolls, but they are both listed in the 'Gay' category on their website, still intended for men's sexual use rather than for a female clientele.

Given that the vast majority of sex dolls and robots are clearly designed with male users in mind – from their pornographic aesthetic to their penetrable orifices – it is clear that when sex doll and robot advocates promote the use of these products as being beneficial for 'people', they mean *male* people. When they claim sex robots could help alleviate loneliness, they mean men's loneliness, not women's. When they argue sex robots could be used by the elderly, they mean elderly men. When they champion the sexual rights of disabled individuals, they mean disabled men. There is little concern for women's suffering, but if men are denied the 'right' to sex on demand, this is framed as deprivation (see Chapter Two).

Sex robots don't technically exist

Sex robots for men's on-demand sexual use are pitched as the potential solution to a number of social issues. Proposals by advocates are – in addition to being premised on male sexual entitlement to the bodies of women and girls – often far-fetched and impractical.

For starters, sex robots – at least in the way they are portrayed in sci-fi films – don't actually exist, and it's unlikely they ever will. In 2010, True Companion claimed to have released Roxxxy, the 'world's first sex robot', but there does not appear to be any evidence Roxxxy actually exists. While creator Douglas Hines claims to have had 4000 orders, nobody seems to have received one (Devlin, 2018, p. 169). Today, the domain name for True Companion's website is for sale.

The sex robots that currently exist are much closer to robotic dolls than sex robots. They have lifelike, silicone sex doll bodies and animatronic heads equipped with artificial intelligence software. Users can pair the robotic head with a smartphone app that functions as a virtual girlfriend (or use the app without a doll). But existing sex robots, or robotic dolls, are very primitive. They cannot walk, or even stand unassisted. Robotic dolls exist that can speak, move, moan or simulate orgasms, and move and blink their eyes. Some have touch sensors and respond to touch, or limited motor function where they can perform a few automated sexual positions, like MISSDOLL's oral sex robot.

Given the rather limited state of sex robot technology, grandiose claims by advocates proclaiming the potential of sex robots to function as intimate partners, to alleviate loneliness or to possibly end sex trafficking, do not seem very plausible. But sex robot advocates continue to speculate on the possible uses of sex robot technology with great confidence.

Reinforcing sexist and racist stereotypes

Most female-bodied sex dolls are fair-skinned, often with white features, but given the sheer volume of options online it is possible to find dolls with the appearance of a variety of different races and ethnicities. Asian dolls are fairly common, as the products are often produced in China and Japan. Black sex dolls are rarer.

Sex doll sellers appear to have taken their cues from the porn industry, with its long history of promoting sexualised and racist stereotypes of people of colour and fetishising their bodies. Black sex dolls are often referred to as 'ebony' sex dolls. Pornhub currently has hundreds of thousands of pornographic videos under search terms like 'ebony', 'ebony big tits', 'big ass ebony', 'ebony milf', 'ebony gangbang', and so forth.

Promotional material for black sex dolls on one sex doll website reads:

> Have you dated a black boyfriend or girlfriend or have you ever imagined having sex with them? Black people tend to have stronger bodies and smoother skin in [sic] the average person, which makes them full of sexy appeal. But now, you can live out your fantasies and fully explore and experiment with your imagination by purchasing a realistic black sex doll (Uloversdoll, 2022).

In promoting black sex dolls, sellers emphasise their dark skin, big butts, 'thick' bodies and big lips. One young-looking black sex doll given the name Betty is described as "a girl from Africa [whose] big lips are better at sucking" (Uloversdoll, 2022). Another, Zara, has a "cinched waist and large bubble butt that loves a good walloping" (Silicon Wives, 2022).

Some promotional material is attributed to dolls themselves. "I hope you like your women thick" is apparently intended from the perspective of a doll named Shanice (Doll Podium, 2022b). Another doll, Amirah, is credited with saying:

> I have a special thing for men who like their women dark, strong and too hot to handle, just like a good cup of espresso! ... I would love to have my big butt whipped and spanked hard (Sex Doll Genie, 2022).

Some black sex dolls are portrayed as animalistic. Makena, "jungle queen," is dressed in a leopard print bikini, described as "one of our thickest and wildest black dolls" (Doll Podium, 2022a).

Online platform Etsy was exposed selling life-size black sex dolls marketed as "Black sex slave." The product description for the sex doll, which comes with three "love holes," reads "sex slave, sex toys for men, fantasy sex toy, women sex toy, sex games, men sex." Images show the doll photographed from behind, naked from the waist down and posed on all fours (Roper, 2022).

Where customers can customise their own dolls and select the skin tone, the options are mainly light-skinned, with one or maybe two black options. Several manufacturers offer to turn any sex doll into a black sex doll.

The acknowledgement that female-bodied sex dolls tend to be modelled on light-skinned women is *not* a call for more diverse representation in sex dolls. Sexually objectifying a wider range of women is not the answer.

Dolls, torsos and body parts

RealDolls are arguably the most famous realistic silicone sex dolls on the market. Manufactured by Abyss Creations, RealDolls have a poseable PVC skeleton and steel joints. As previously outlined, they are mostly embodied female, although there are a couple of male-bodied dolls. Dolls can be purchased as is, with options like Stephanie, Willow or Tanya, or they can be customised. Buyers can build their own ideal woman, choosing from a range of different faces, body types, skin tones, eye colours, makeup styles, hairstyles and colours, breasts, custom nipples and vaginal inserts. They can also opt for extras, like customisable freckles or piercings, or a Transgender Converter – a silicone penis that "will turn your RealDoll into a transgender whenever you feel like it, without being a permanent switch" for an extra $500.

Wicked RealDolls are made in the likeness of famous female porn performers, built from moulds of their bodies. They are promoted on the RealDoll website as follows:

> Tired of simply dreaming about your favorite porn model? No need to fantasize alone imagining the company of your special leading lady. Wicked RealDoll brings your favorite star out from behind the screen and into your bedsheets for a wild night unlike any other … With a Wicked RealDoll, you can finally spend a night with your dream girl whenever you feel like it (RealDoll, 2018).

In addition to full-sized dolls, the company also offers a range of accessories, including magnetic faces (so users can alternate their doll faces for variety), disembodied feet, and oral simulators – silicone replicas of the bottom half of a woman's face, with red, glossy, parted lips – to replicate the experience of fellatio.

For those on a budget, there are also headless torsos available. The Female Deluxe RealDoll Torso is modelled on the torso of a woman – with pornified features – but has no arms or legs. The Deluxe Half Torso is a replica of a woman's buttocks, bent over as though in preparation to be penetrated from behind. Users can select their preferred vaginal insert, including options modelled on the bodies of female porn performers.

The Insert Facilitator Torso looks like a woman's disembodied pelvic region, cropped just above the belly button and with no legs. Verified buyers praise the product's realism. Gary M writes:

The Insert Facilitator Torso has been a real blessing to me. As a single man who simply wanted a way to satisfy my needs without spending thousands of dollars this torso was the perfect solution. I've tried other simulated vagina products and none of them even come close to the look and real feel of this torso. It's always there and always ready. Want sweet relief that feels like the real thing? Buy this torso. You will be very pleased you did (RealDoll, 2020).

The Bottoms-up Male is the only torso modelled on a man's body, depicting a man bent over from behind, up to the waist, with legs cut off but anus and scrotum visible. The (eight inch deep) penetrable anal orifice suggests that this product, too, is intended for a male market.

Sex dolls as stand-ins for women

But while there is a market for disembodied body parts, it is the representation of dolls as 'real' women that holds the most appeal. Dolls are typically marketed not as sex toys, but as though they are real women. They are even portrayed as potential companions, with the ability to meet users' emotional needs.

A promotional video for AI Tech's humanoid sex robot, 'Emma', portrays it not as a sexual product, but as an intimate partner (coco quin, 2017). In the video, a man is shown lying in bed, surrounded by empty bottles and rubbish. He is alone, and his life is joyless. Then, the doorbell rings – it is 'Emma' the sex robot, who arrives in a coffin-like box, and suddenly everything is better.

With soft piano music playing in the background, the man is depicted in romantic scenarios with his sex robot – on a picnic, lying in the sunshine and cuddling the robot among the wildflowers. The camera pans over him lying in bed next to 'Emma', fast asleep but with a smile on his face. Despite being an object, 'Emma' the sex robot is portrayed as being able to meet his emotional needs and fill the role of female partner.

A voiceover at the end of the video says, "Love is the foundation of success. True love can never be silent. Shenzen AI Tech creates the perfect girlfriend who knows you best."

Fiona Andreallo, Lecturer in Digital Culture at the University of Sydney notes:

> [D]espite the tone of these ads, the imagery in the marketing of Emma is sexualised and reminiscent of soft-core pornography. She [sic] is clearly addressed to a heterosexual man. She might be marketed as a companion, but she is a companion for a very specific demographic (Andreallo, 2019).

Promotional material for robotic sex dolls on DS Dolls' website is one example of many where sex dolls are likened to a female partner, only better:

> An artificial intelligent robot girlfriend experience can be as realistic as a date with a hot girl, and a great deal cheaper in the long run ... The eco-friendly, non-toxic platinum silicone sex dolls have hanging hooks available to allow you to store her away when you don't want to play.

> When you're in the mood for some adult fun, a DS Doll synthetic woman is always sexually available. There's no need to spend a fortune trying to impress your date. You just need to get her out and dress her up in whatever takes your fancy ... Should you ever desire a change of partner, you can simply switch her interchangeable head (DS Doll Robotics, 2021).

Sex doll brothel websites portray dolls just as they would living women, divided into categories such as 'Blonde', 'Latina', 'Big Boobs', and 'MILF' (Mother I'd Like to Fuck). On some sites, dolls have individual profiles in the style of dating profiles. Sex doll 'Katarina' is promoted as a 32-year-old stewardess from Kazakhstan now living in London. 'Tiffany' grew up in a conservative family, studied Economics and loves to cook. A doll given the name 'Either' shares her backstory as a psychologist who specialises in sexology, along with a few paragraphs outlining her philosophies on life and sex.

Sex dolls: The literal objectification of women

Sexual objectification occurs when a person (usually a woman) is made into a thing for someone else's sexual use (usually a man). Female-bodied sex dolls and robots represent the literal objectification of women. They are objects to be used in place of women. They are embodied representations of women designed purely for men's sexual gratification, manufactured for the express purpose of being sexually used.

That a piece of silicone in the shape of a woman could be seen as an acceptable replacement for a human woman – or even superior to an actual woman – demonstrates how too many men view women: as less than human, or at least not human in the way men are human, but rather as the means to fulfil their sexual gratification, a set of holes to provide sexual relief whenever required.

Being reduced to the status of object has a range of significant negative effects on women and girls. The harmful impacts from sexualising and objectifying representations of women in mainstream media have been well established over decades of research. A review of 20 years of empirical research, 135 studies across 109 publications, found that

> regular, everyday exposure to [sexually objectifying portrayals of women] are directly associated with a range of consequences, including higher levels of body dissatisfaction, greater self-objectification, greater support of sexist beliefs and of adversarial sexual beliefs, and greater tolerance of sexual violence toward women. Moreover, experimental exposure to this content leads both women and men to have a diminished view of women's competence, morality, and humanity (Ward, 2016, p. 560).

Objectification has been linked to men's violence against women. In *Refusing to be a Man: Essays on Sex and Justice*, John Stoltenberg explains how sexual objectification can serve as a justification for violence against women:

> There is a perceptible sense in which every act of sexual objectifying occurs on a continuum of dehumanization that promises

male violence at its far end. The depersonalisation that begins in sexual objectification is what makes violence possible; for once you have made a person out to be a thing, you can do anything you want (Stoltenberg, 2000, p. 45).

The erosion of consent

Female-bodied sex dolls and robots that are always ready and available for men's sexual use portray women's consent to sexual acts as irrelevant.

A sex doll has no needs to be met, no free will to be exercised, and no expectation of an equal or mutually beneficial partnership. It is a manufactured product that exists solely to provide sexual pleasure for its user, predicated on men's absolute sexual freedom without limits. There is no pressure to perform well, no need to reciprocate, no need to consider the other party's feelings, enjoyment, discomfort, humiliation or pain. It facilitates the embodied fantasy experience of sex with a compliant woman that is all about the user's sexual fantasies – with a woman who never refuses, and can be used over and over again.

Dolls and robots can neither give nor refuse consent, as they are objects, not women. But as they are embodied female, and constantly sexually available, they function as non-sentient female sex slaves:

> By design, sex robots do not have the ability to complain or reject the user. To the user, the sex robot looks and feels like a real woman who is programmed into submission and which functions as a tool for sexual purposes. The sex robot is an ever-consenting sexual partner and the user has full control of the robot and the sexual interaction (Gutiu, 2012, p. 2).

Sex dolls and robots undermine established social norms around consent. As endlessly available sexual 'partners', the use of sex robots may lead to an understanding of consent as a one-time achievement. Men's use of female-bodied sex dolls and robots could result in what lawyer Sinziana Gutiu describes as the "erosion of consent" (2016, p. 202) by affecting users' ability to understand and recognise when consent is present in sexual interactions, and teaching them that when it comes to consent, "only no means no" (p. 209).

When men use sex dolls and robots made in the likeness of women, they do not have to obtain or even consider consent – they are concerned only with their own pleasure. Through their use of sex dolls and robots, consent becomes irrelevant, rather than a necessary component of a sexual encounter with another party. It is worth contemplating how a man who has repeatedly practiced this sexual dynamic on a doll might relate sexually to a woman.

Sex robots programmed to outright refuse consent and facilitate rape fantasies have attracted significant controversy and media attention. At this stage, though, such products probably do not exist. True Companion's sex robot Roxxxy was reported as coming with several pre-programmed personalities for users to choose from: 'Wild Wendy', 'S & M Susan', 'Mature Martha', 'Frigid Farrah' or 'Young Yoko'. 'Frigid Farrah' was marketed as being "reserved and shy" and "if touched in a private area [will] more than likely … not be appreciative of your advance." Roxxxy appears to be a myth, but as development continues, it is inevitable that similar products will be released.

Of course, it is not necessary to have a robotic doll that protests in order for men to use dolls to experiment with and practice rape. A sex doll, which replicates the body of an unconscious woman who cannot resist, is already a viable option.

Sex dolls as a backlash against women's rights

The development of sex dolls and robots in the female form represents a backlash against women's political gains. While the women's movement has achieved some success, sex dolls and robots reduce women to sexual objects, and reassert men's dominance over them.

It's no accident that most sex dolls are made in the female form. Hideo Tsuchiya, president of Tokyo-based sex doll company Orient Industry, said not only that nearly all of their customers were single men, but that the dolls were produced in response to women's increased 'dominance':

> Nowadays, women are sometimes more dominant than men in the real world, and they don't always pay attention to men. More and more men are finding themselves miserable so we're making these dolls partly in support of men (Maeda, 2007).

Sex dolls and robots represent an underlying threat to women – fall in line or be replaced. A number of video sketches shared on Instagram follow this theme, depicting women being replaced by sex robots as punishment for being 'bad' wives. In one clip, a woman is portrayed as 'nagging' her husband to do the laundry, so he replaces her with a sex robot. The robot is identical to his wife, but superior on the basis it has no mind of its own and is always available for sex.

In another video, a woman tells her partner she is dissatisfied with their sex life. He responds, "I got something just like you that don't complain," and proceeds to show her a sex robot that looks just like her, but performs sex acts on demand.

In a YouTube video entitled *Women Are In Trouble In 2018 Lmao* [Laugh my Ass off], comedian Ryan Davis encourages men to turn to a sex doll if their female partner 'acts up':

> This one won't go through your phone. I don't have to remember her birthday, Valentine's Day, Christmas, ain't never gotta meet her parents, ain't never gotta worry about what she been doing all day – she been in the closet where I left her, all day ... And she never gets her period. Ever. She's always in the mood, because she don't [sic] have moods ... I'm buying one today. Fellas, we not arguing with these women in 2018, man. When they start acting up, we're like, 'I don't need this! I got a bad chick under my bed right now, I'll pull that out' (With All Due Offense, 2018).

Men's rights activists, a group of men who believe men are socially disadvantaged and who openly oppose women's rights, see female-bodied sex dolls as a wake-up call to women who have forgotten their place and fail to treat men with the respect they deserve. On MRA websites and forums, these men refer to women as cunts and argue their only value is in providing sexual gratification. MRAs believe women's objections to sex dolls are based on fears they are losing their 'power' over men. As one man wrote on online forum A Voice for Men, "Sex is really the only power women have over men, and that is what they fear, losing that power." As MRAs see it, women are "scared of competition" and "starting to sweat."

According to MRAs, sex dolls and robots render women obsolete. The availability of sex dolls means women can be replaced, and if men can purchase a sex doll, they no longer have any need for living women. One user on A Voice for Men wrote, "These machines can satisfy [men's] one primary need that keeps them tied to women." In a Men Going Their Own Way (MGTOW) forum, one user wrote:

> Remember that old joke? Question – What's the definition of a woman? Answer – A life support system for a cunt.

> With sex-bots and exo-wombs, we're on the cusp of developing a better life support system for cunts. Imagine, a meathole that doesn't nag, make demands, or pass along STDs ... Women will become obsolete.

MRAs argue sex dolls and robots are far superior to living women, and owning a sex doll allows men to avoid the burdens of a relationship with a woman.

> For a man who wants to live the fantasy of being in a relationship without any of the hassle and risk, I would bet sex dolls are the way to go. They're expensive, but you'd have to spend much more on a meatbag hoe.

Unlike women, sex dolls are always sexually available, and never say no:

Both robots and modern women can't cook but at least the robot spreads the legs every time.

If you can just buy a sexbot, why do you want to put up with the woman that comes attached to the vagina?

Sex dolls are a better option than women. There really isn't much difference in terms of what they offer, but the sex doll will give it to you 100% of the time, no questions asked.

Sex dolls also remain fuckable, unlike real women who age or might gain weight.

[A] decent sex doll is more attractive than most women. Most women are too fat and unattractive to be worth screwing, and their personalities make them doubly unattractive.

Women are useful in only one way: as cum receptacles. That is the only value they offer, what they have made themselves. Everything else they do is useless, if not detrimental to society. If that's the only thing they have to offer, why not get a sex doll that does it better, and then forget about women forever? It's perfect, you get to have a better version of a woman with none of the downsides.

Unlike women, sex dolls have no limits on their use, they have no autonomy, and they can't speak.

I think the best thing about a female sex bot is that it will come with an adjustable volume knob and a mute button. That alone is worth the price of admission.

One thing for sure, these robots won't have the word 'rape' in their vocabulary.

Sex or masturbation: Conceptualising men's sex doll use

Female-bodied dolls marketed for men's sexual use are commonly known as sex dolls or sex robots, but what is being done by men is not exactly *sex*. Dolls, even robotic ones, are objects. They do not have sexed bodies, nor do they have consciousness. There can be

21

no relationship, which requires mutuality, with an object one owns – even if it is programmed to give the illusion or appearance of reciprocity. It is impossible to 'have sex' with an inanimate object.

In order to have sex, a sentient partner is required – a subject, not an object. According to philosophers Mark Migotti and Nicole Wyatt, sex is

> what you have with all and only your sexual partners ... for sex to be had – we maintain – there must be a sexual we having it [sic]. If having sex requires shared sexual agency, it really does take (at least) two to tango ... Sex props are mere objects; sex partners are also subjects in their own right (Migotti and Wyatt, 2017, p. 16, 20, 21).

When men sexually use dolls, it is a one-sided sexual experience. It is not sex, it is masturbation.

Advocates for sex dolls and robots dismiss objections to the products on this basis – that their use is the equivalent of masturbation. If sex dolls and robots simply aid masturbation, and if they are nothing more than sophisticated sex toys, then theoretically, they do not raise any unique ethical issues:

> As long as these robots remain non-sentient, elaborate masturbatory aids, we estimate no significant, negative impact on society (Klein and Wenli Lin, 2018, p. 121).

If sex dolls and robots are conceptualised as mere sex toys to facilitate masturbation – which is how advocates frame them – it could be argued any regulation or criminalisation would be inappropriate. This is the argument put forth by defenders of child sex abuse dolls like the US-based organisation Prostasia Foundation, which describes men's use of child-like dolls as "the personal and private use of sex toys" and argues laws against them are unconstitutional (Prostasia Foundation, 2019).

But sex dolls and robots are fundamentally different from standard sex toys. They are embodied in human form – typically, the female form. They look and feel like a woman. They are designed to emulate a realistic experience of sex with a woman, one who is endlessly sexually available.

Sex doll manufacturers promote dolls as substitutes for women. They emphasise the dolls' realism. For example, RealDoll's name and slogan on its website front page: "Nothing beats the real thing." Doll sellers actively encourage users to form emotional attachments to them. Unlike typical sex toys, female-bodied sex dolls and robots are humanised, usually given names, and sometimes even personalities and backstories by manufacturers.

Female-bodied sex dolls are not sex toys like any other, as they are modelled on, and replicate, the bodies of women and children. They are representations of women and girls to be used in their place; lifelike replica women and girls produced to be sexually used by men without limitations. As PhD candidate and sex tech researcher Chloé Locatelli explains:

> The expectation, and desire, that a sex toy as object should be constantly able to satisfy sexual desires is not in itself problematic, but, when this is gendered-female and sold as a product with the capacity to emulate an ideal of 'woman' – an ideal implying constant sexual availability – the ethics of it must be seriously investigated (Locatelli, 2018, p. 62).

Defenders of sex dolls and robots argue that no one is harmed by men's use of them, because they are objects. But these objects are used as stand-ins for women and children, so what men do to them matters.

Not just a fantasy

Advocates for men's access to sex dolls and robots, including those made in the likeness of children, characterise the products as "fantasy sexual outlets" (Prostasia Foundation, n.d.). But men's sexual use of replica women and children is not merely fantasy. As Andrea Dworkin pointed out, fantasy occurs in the mind:

> A fantasy is something that happens in your head. It doesn't go
> past your head. Once you have somebody acting out whatever
> that scenario might be in your head, it is an act in the world. It is
> real (Dworkin, n.d.).

When men purchase and perform sex acts on a doll, they have
moved from the realm of fantasy to behaviour; these are real acts
in the world.

While the 'fantasy' may be that the replica woman or child they
are penetrating is an actual woman, or an actual child, the sex act is
real – not a simulation, and not a fantasy. As feminist scholar Rae
Langton writes, whether it is a piece of paper, a doll or a virtual
human being, the attribution of humanity is make believe, but the
sexual experience is real:

> When someone treats a thing as a human being, in a sexual
> context, he does not believe outright it is a human being, but
> he may act as if it were. He may talk with it, he may praise it,
> or blame it; he may attribute to the thing beliefs about himself,
> and desires. He may direct a range of reactive attitudes towards
> it. And he has sex with it. The talk, praise, blame, belief/desire
> attribution, is in some sense make-believe. The sexual experience
> is not (Langton, 2009, p. 314).

Theorising men's consumption of pornography, legal scholar
Catharine MacKinnon argued that male consumers are participating in a real – not imagined – sex act, one that takes place in their
bodies and not just their minds. Their erections are real, and their
orgasms are real (MacKinnon, 1993, p. 17). Feminist philosopher
Melinda Vadas similarly noted that while consuming pornography,
men experience the same physiological markers they would during
sex, beginning with sexual arousal and ending with orgasm and
ejaculation. Men's consumption of pornography is not merely
fantasy or a simulated sex act, it is a real sex act, "an act no other
sex act is realer than" (Vadas, 2005, p. 179).

Likewise, men who use sex dolls and robots are performing a
real sex act, on a realistic replica woman or child. It is possible the

embodied experience of using a doll, in contrast with masturbating to pornography, could provide an even more powerful sensory experience, further reinforcing this behaviour.

It is also worth noting that men's 'fantasies' for sexually using and abusing women and children, acted out on lifelike dolls, occur within a wider culture where such sexualised abuse is not a fantasy, but a reality for many women and girls. Men's 'fantasies' are women's lived experiences.

Rape and necrophilia

Men's use of sex dolls has also been likened to acts of rape and necrophilia. Artist and Lecturer in Fine Art, Shirley MacWilliam, describes sex dolls and robots as "dead body objects," with a sex doll as a "dead woman" and a sex robot as an "animated corpse" (MacWilliam, forthcoming). In an essay, feminist geographer, Lydia Delicado-Moratalla (forthcoming) argues that, given non-reciprocal sexual intercourse with an unconscious woman constitutes rape, using a sex doll is more closely aligned with rape than sex. When men who own sex dolls take and distribute pornographic content of themselves using their lifeless dolls – a common pastime on sex doll user forums – it is a representation of rape.

> The female replica is expected to act as an immobilised frozen body while being penetrated …The scenes not only mimic the sexual subordination of women to men, but also show that all control is held by the male actor with no possibility for the female to object. Doll consumers act as if 'sexually' using completely realistic representations of unconscious women – and sometimes underage girls – is acceptable (Delicado-Moratalla, forthcoming).

Sex doll users and advocates claim there is no harm in enacting rape or abuse on female-bodied dolls because they are not hurting a real woman or girl, but as Delicado-Moratalla points out,

... they are, in fact, harming women indirectly because they are creating a narrative that builds from the symbolic abuse of women ... This metaphoric use of rape representations is problematic because it sets the conditions for accepting rape as something desirable (Delicado-Moratalla, forthcoming).

These representations of rape are harmful because they portray rape as desirable,

[sharing and uploading] sets of pro-rape images, fantasies that travel through internet networks without any critical approach. These rape-devotional sexual masculinities become thus visible, popular and mainstream, creating room for their validation and constructing unsafe social spaces for women ... [T]his content has the ability to influence others, because it is being reproduced hundreds of times with every visualisation and download (Delicado-Moratalla, forthcoming).

Sex dolls and robots as 3D porn

Female-bodied sex dolls and robots can be understood as three-dimensional, potentially interactive pornography. Dolls are typically designed according to pornographic standards, intended to mimic the surgically enhanced bodies and appearance of female porn performers. Sex dolls facilitate a form of pornography male users can actively participate in, an embodied experience where they themselves can be both actors and pornographers.

Through their use of sex dolls, men replicate the same power dynamics eroticised in pornography – male dominance and female subordination. Pornography is premised on the sexual objectification of women. Women's bodies and sexuality are commodified as things for someone else's sexual use. They are presented "dehumanised as sexual objects, things, or commodities" (Dworkin, 1981, p. xxxiii). In pornography, men are human and women are objects.

Indeed, the concept of woman as object is "at the very core of the pornographic mise-en-scène", writes radical feminist philosopher, Susan Griffin, in *Pornography and Silence: Culture's Revenge against Nature* (1981, p. 32).

> A *being* exists only in order to exist. For a woman or a man exists no *particular* material purpose. But a thing, an object, must have a reason for being, a function. And where the pornographic 'woman' is concerned, that function is to please a man ... *She* exists for *his* pleasure (p. 32).

In pornography, women play the part of object to be mastered and controlled:

> Not only does a woman exist to serve and to please; but in this subordinate existence of hers she has no rights whatsoever, for she does not belong to herself (p. 34).

The pornographer loves the body of the woman, "her flesh alone" but has no interest in her soul (p. 33).

Griffin also identifies sex dolls as a form of pornography – the "pornographic doll," she explains, is "the pornographic object's most quintessential form." Griffin defines a pornographic doll as "an actual plastic copy of a woman, made to replace a woman, and to give a man pleasure *without the discomfort of female presence*" (p. 36, italics added). She outlines the appeal of such dolls to the pornographic mind, "Her vagina opens 'on command', she is 'ready to go, night after night', she does not talk back, she is perfectly controllable" (p. 36).

In pornography, not only are women treated as objects, objects are treated as women (MacKinnon, 1993; Vadas, 2005). MacKinnon writes that in pornography, "human becomes thing" (1993, p. 106). What this means is in pornography people, usually women, are objectified and treated as things to be sexually used. It also means pornography, in the form of words and pictures – things – is used as a woman. Men use pornography, a thing, in place of a female sexual partner. Their consumption of pornography is "sex between people and things, human beings and pieces of paper, real men and unreal women" (MacKinnon, 1993, p. 140). Vadas, too, argues that when men consume pornography they are using it "as a woman," or as a stand in for a woman (Vadas, 2005, p. 177).

When men use pornography, a manufactured object, *as a woman* or in place of a woman, this has consequences for women's status. As Langton writes:

> When sex is something you do with a thing ... it becomes something you do with a thing, even when you do it with a person. When you treat things as human beings, you end up treating human beings as things (Langton, 2009, p. 348).

If objects can be used in place of women, then women and objects are interchangeable. If pornography – an object – is used as a woman, Vadas theorises, a new category of reality is created, comprised of both "flesh and blood women" (p. 189) and the female "pornographic object" (p. 177). Women exist in the same category as objects, which means women are not necessarily persons and personhood is not a necessary property of women. If women are non-persons, their sexual identity is therefore constructed as rapable and their consent to sexual activity becomes irrelevant (Vadas, 2005).

When men use a female-bodied sex doll or robot, they are using it *as a woman*, or in place of a woman. Through men's sex doll use, women become interchangeable with dolls, and are relegated to the status of objects.

CHAPTER TWO

Sex robots as the solution to men's sexual 'deprivation'

Are you lonely? A sex robot could be the answer.

Grieving the death of an intimate partner? A sex robot made in the likeness of your dead spouse could be just the thing.

Struggling to grasp the concept of sexual consent? A sex robot might help.

Going on a space mission and no one around to fuck? You need a sex robot!

One of the more common narratives utilised in defence of sex dolls and robots is that they could provide 'companionship' and comfort to 'people' – at least, the kind with penises – who are lonely, who are grieving the death of a loved one, who struggle with social anxiety or are faced with some other barrier that might prevent them from forming intimate relationships with other people.

The notion that sex dolls or robots could cure loneliness could not be further from the truth. Like the consumption of pornography, where the user masturbates to a screen, sex dolls and robots facilitate a one-sided, disconnected, solo sexual experience. In both cases, there is no partner – just woman-as-object to provide sexual gratification. The user remains alone, no matter how much he might like to pretend otherwise.

In this context, screens, objects and machines do not promote intimacy and connection, they increase alienation. They function as obstacles that prevent humans from connecting with other humans. The sexual dynamic inherent in sex doll use is not premised on connection or empathy, it is based on the view of sex as a purely physical experience, as nothing more than the means of sexual release, with women existing to facilitate it. It is not a mutual experience between two people, but rather man and woman-as-object.

Having established that these 'people' are typically men, the argument that a female-bodied sex doll or robot could cure men's loneliness is nonsensical. A sex doll or robot is an inanimate object, a thing – not a human being. There can be no *relationship*, which requires mutuality, with an object one owns.

At best, technological advancements in sex robots could eventually result in a robotic doll that is programmed to more convincingly mimic a woman and provide the illusion of recip-rocity, but there is no authentic intimacy involved in the process of sexually penetrating a machine.

Sex dolls and robots are not women, they are objects used in place of a woman. The notion that a piece of silicone in the shape of a woman could function as a stand-in for a woman is premised on the belief that a woman is reduceable to her sexual functions; that she is a 'thing' that exists to be sexually used by men.

A sex doll or robot – an object – could only be seen to be interchangeable with a woman *if women themselves are regarded as objects*. In encouraging men's use of sex dolls and robots as an alternative to relationships with women, sex doll and robot advocates reveal how they see women – as objects for men's sexual gratification.

The fact that a pornified female-bodied doll with penetrable orifices, endlessly available for men's sexual use, is portrayed as the means for alleviating loneliness suggests it is not actual intimacy or connection being sought, as a sex doll can provide neither. What is being sought, however, is sex on demand.

I do have compassion for those who suffer through loneliness – male or female – who would like to have a partner in life and for whatever reason have not found one. But I strongly reject the claim made by sex doll and robot advocates that a piece of silicone in the shape of a person can alleviate human needs for intimacy and connection. And even if it could, it would still not be a justification for the dehumanisation of half the population.

As this chapter will show, there is no shortage of advocates proclaiming the supposed benefits of sex robot technology (for men). But there is very little consideration of the potential consequences for women and girls.

Advocates fail to explore how pornified dolls modelled on the bodies of women and girls and marketed for men's sexual use pose a threat to the status of women. They neglect to consider how female-bodied sex robots could further entrench sexist attitudes towards women, contribute to rape culture and encourage men's violence against women and girls. Advocates seem to be more concerned with the potential benefits for men than the harms to women and girls.

These advocates are mostly men who remain very committed to the production of, and men's access to, sex dolls and robots modelled on the bodies of women – and sometimes, children.

Sex robot advocates

The most well-known proponent of sex robots is David Levy. In his 2007 book, *Love and Sex with Robots*, Levy made bold predictions for the future of human-robot relations, including that by 2050, humans will be falling in love with, and marrying, sex robots. He had originally claimed this could be happening as soon as 2025, but has since revised the date.

Levy poses a range of possible uses for sex robots: intimate partners for those who have lost a partner to death, illness or a broken relationship; as an alternative to paying for sex, suggesting a prostitute-client relationship dynamic (a point I will return to in Chapter Four); and as outlets for those who wish to engage in what he loosely terms "illegal and antisocial sexual practices" (Levy, 2007a, p. 308).

According to Levy, sex robots will be welcomed not just by men, but by women too, because women use vibrators: "Anyone who has doubts that women will find [sex robots] appealing ... should think again. Think vibrators" (p. 220). Sex robots will provide both companionship and "great sex on tap for everyone, 24/7," Levy promises (p. 310).

Levy is not alone. There are a number of sex robot advocates, both inside and outside of academia, who claim sex robots will revolutionise our sex lives and contribute to better health, wellbeing and quality of life. While some advocates take a gender-neutral approach, and others claim sex robots could be embraced by women too, it is evident that their proposals are overwhelmingly made with a male consumer in mind.

Sexual rights and disability

Advocates for sexual rights believe that sex is a fundamental human right – not merely masturbation, but sex with another person.

Bioethicist Jacob M. Appel argues that because the pleasure from partnered sex is both distinct from and greater than that of masturbation, "if any right to sexual pleasure does exist ... then it must be a right to mutual contact, not merely self-stimulation" (Appel, 2010, p. 152). If sex with another person is a human right, then someone else must be made available to meet that need.

In the academic literature, the notion of sexual rights typically refers to the sexual rights of men, which can be understood as men's sexual access to women's bodies. The sex trade is frequently justified on the basis of men's sexual rights; that men need sex, and without it they would be lonely, suffering and sexually deprived. In particular, men with disabilities and their sexual 'rights' have long been invoked as a justification for the sex industry, allowing sex trade profiteers to paint men's paid sexual access to the bodies of women as a compassionate service rather than a system of male violence against vulnerable women and girls.

Sexual rights advocates campaign for disabled men's access to pornography and prostitution, though, as feminist scholar Sheila Jeffreys points out, gender is never referred to in the literature which is "carefully neutral" (Jeffreys, 2008, p. 331). Research on disability and sexuality usually does not disaggregate the interests of women with disabilities from those of men with disabilities, yet disabled men "may pursue interests that are in stark contradiction to those of disabled women," Jeffreys notes (p. 327). Much of this data takes a gender-neutral approach, referring to 'people' with disabilities or disabled 'individuals', while still having a "male body and sexuality in mind" (p. 327).[1]

A number of academics have argued that physically and mentally disabled 'individuals' should be permitted to pay for sex, or even that they should be entitled to subsidised prostitution and 'sexual surrogacy' sessions. The sex of these individuals who are arguably entitled to sex is not mentioned, but given the gendered nature of the sex industry, with sellers being primarily women and buyers overwhelmingly men, it is likely these academics have a "male body and sexuality in mind."

Researcher Ezio di Nucci (2011) offers an alternative approach, proposing charitable non-profits whose members would, in theory, voluntarily and freely provide sexual pleasure to the severely disabled. Like others, Di Nucci does not specify the sex of the disabled individuals who are entitled to sexual servicing, nor the sex of the volunteers who would be expected to make themselves available to cheerfully do the sexual servicing, leaving readers to draw their own conclusions.

---

1   See also Sheila Jeffreys, *Penile Imperialism: The Male Sex Right and Women's Subordination*, Spinifex Press, 2022.

Brian D. Earp and Ole Martin Moen (2016) go even further, arguing that prostitution should be legal and accessible for everyone, not just those who are disabled. There are a range of reasons why "all sorts of people," including those deemed unattractive, or who are shy or socially awkward, may struggle to form sexual relationships, and prostitution should be an option for all of them (p. 2). But then there are also those who are perceived as very attractive, who have no problems in social settings, but who have an "insatiable sexual appetite." These individuals too, they argue, should be allowed to pay for sex, as they may struggle to find "enough willing sexual partners ... to 'satisfy' their 'needs'" (p. 2).

Given, as outlined above, sex industry sellers are primarily women, and it is predominantly men, not women, who are customers of the sex industry, Earp and Moen's call for accessible prostitution for everyone can be read as a call for *men's* paid sexual access to the bodies of *women* in the sex trade. Not just men who are disabled, or who are 'deprived' of sex, but even those having plenty of sex but who still want more, or who want it on their terms or under their control. The rhetoric of sexual rights emboldens men in their entitlement to sex at any time, in any way that they want it, and in their belief that anything less constitutes sexual deprivation – a violation of their rights.

Disability and sex robots

Sexual rights advocates have seized upon the potential for sex robot technology as the answer to men's apparent sexual deprivation, i.e. not getting sex however and whenever they want it. According to di Nucci, sex robots allow for the sexual 'rights' of users to be met without having to violate another person's rights, who would otherwise have to allow the use of their body for the user's sexual gratification (2017, p. 73).

Pro-sex robot academics call for sex robots to be made available for use by the elderly and physically and mentally disabled. When it comes to individuals who are disabled, di Nucci, like a number of others, extols the "great health and wellbeing benefits" from masturbating into a sex robot. He argues that while "avoidance may be the *safer* option for us ... it would not be the *just* one for anybody" (pp. 85–86). In other words, not only would sex robots benefit disabled users, but failing to provide them would be harmful.

The proposals for sex robots for the elderly and disabled are, like proposals for the products more generally, often unrealistic and neglect practical considerations e.g. the fact that sex robots do not technically exist, or that lifelike RealDolls even without any robotic element start at about $6000 each. Sex robot advocates also often fail to consider the range of ethical issues involved, including how the 'rights' of individuals to use sex robots might conflict with the rights of their carers (often female) who will be required to assist and clean up after.

Researcher Nancy Jecker makes a 'dignity-based' argument for providing sex robots for the elderly: "a society which supports human dignity must take seriously the claims of those who lose the ability to be sexual and must make reasonable efforts to help" (Jecker, 2021, pp. 26–27). Indeed, she continues, to "shun a person's sexual behaviour" (i.e. failing to provide them with a sex robot), "conveys a lack of respect for persons" (p. 28). This "respect for persons," however, does not extend to men enacting rape fantasies on robots, which Jecker declares is "none of anyone else's business" (p. 31). Sex robots for the elderly could be modelled on a deceased spouse, or old film stars like Bette Davis or Sidney Poitier, Jecker posits.

Jecker argues that while many people with disabilities are capable of masturbation, the ultimate desire is for a sexual relationship, which can be found in a sex robot. Unlike other aids designed to enhance sexual activity, she asserts, sex robots simulate sex with another person and involve forming a human-robot relationship, and "can be a lifeline to human intimacy" (p. 30).

But there is no human intimacy involved in using a sex robot – the sexual use of a robot constitutes neither *human* nor *intimacy*.

Sex robots are objects, and as such, there is no relationship. There can be no mutuality, no reciprocity – only imitation, the illusion of reciprocity. Indeed, masturbating into an object in the shape of a person – typically a woman – is in stark contrast with human connection or intimacy.

Jecker argues sex robots should be made available for the elderly in support of human dignity, but fails to consider the dignity of women, caricatured as pornified dolls with huge, cartoonish breasts and removable vaginal inserts. It would appear men's sexual 'rights' take precedence over women's rights to dignity and equality.

How sex robots will improve (men's) sex lives

Some researchers claim sex robot technology could revolutionise our sex lives, bringing a range of benefits: providing sex education and helping people to become better lovers, improving intimate relationships and contributing to overall health, wellbeing and happiness.

Simon Dubé, a PhD candidate who specialises in Erobotics – the study of human and machine erotic interaction – claims that sex robot technology can help people become "better erotic beings" by teaching users to become "better lovers and sexual partners":

> This technology can be used and designed to help us understand each other and improve the quality of our relationships with fellow humans ... We need machines to learn what our sexual preferences are and nudge us in the right direction (Dubé, 2021 as quoted in Pettit, 2021).

But Dubé's proposal raises a number of questions. For starters, why is a machine needed for a person to figure out what they like sexually? How does sexually penetrating a machine prepare someone for, or improve their relationship with, an actual human – someone with their own thoughts, feelings and desires, and not merely a lifeless receptacle for semen? And how does masturbating into a silicone doll make one a more attentive intimate partner?

In addition to claims sex robots could teach people to be better lovers, some advocates argue they could even strengthen intimate partnerships.

According to Neil McArthur, Associate Professor of Philosophy at the University of Manitoba, sex robots could be the solution to 'desire discrepancy', where one partner has a greater sex drive than the other, leading to friction in the relationship. A sex robot could provide an outlet for the partner with the higher sex drive and therefore "strengthen the relationship" (2017, p. 41) by relieving resentment in the higher sex drive partner and relieving pressure or guilt in the other.

Based on the accounts of women whose husbands preferred their dolls to having sex with them (see Chapter Five), the notion sex dolls could enhance intimate relationships seems unlikely.

Having a sex robot constantly available for use could also allow individuals who wish to indulge in sadistic sexual practices the opportunity to do so whenever the mood strikes, again taking pressure off their partner, McArthur argues.

McArthur does not specify the sex of the partner who might require a sex robot to accommodate their high sex drive, or on which to practice sadistic sex acts. Nor does he specify the sex of the partner who might feel pressured to submit to unwanted or abusive sex acts, or be expected to tolerate their partner owning and using a sex robot.

Sex dolls and robots provide men with the means for more *selfish* sex – 'sex' that is totally one-sided. It is 'sex' predicated on men's absolute sexual freedom to dominate and use a woman without limitations. Dolls – inanimate objects – do not facilitate intimacy and human connection; they are barriers to it.

While this particular 'relationship' dynamic will certainly appeal to some men, it won't make them better sexual partners – or improve their real-life relationships.

How sex robots will improve (men's) health

A number of sex robot advocates claim the products could improve users' health, wellbeing and happiness on the basis that sex is good, and more of it is better. In *The Case for Sexbots*, McArthur (2017) argues most people consider sex to be a good thing rather than a bad thing, that having more sex is better than having less sex, and that sex robots could be the means to people having more sex. Essentially, the development of sex robots could increase the potential for sexual satisfaction and "overall happiness" (p. 34) – and society will "end up better off for it" (p. 32):

> The invention of sex robots will not be just morally neutral, but will in fact be, on balance, a positive good. I am advocating not just that we tolerate them, but that we actively encourage their development, support their distribution, and work to overcome stigmas associated with them (p. 33).

In a 2018 review, Nicola Döring and Sandra Pöschl expressed similar sentiments, concluding that sex robots could offer sexual pleasure and fulfilment, leading to wellbeing and improved quality of life.

Döring and Pöschl conducted a review of sex toys, sex dolls and sex robots, which they grouped together as "sexual products" despite obvious differences. They examined self-reports from users of the various products, who reported experiencing sexual and emotional satisfaction from them. On this basis – that users of sex dolls and robots found the experience to be sexually pleasurable – Döring and Pöschl encouraged health professionals to normalise their use and called for further development:

> Instead of just criticizing dystopian visions of harmful sex robots, why not make a joint effort to develop robots with positive impact in terms of sex education, sexual therapy, sexual counseling and sexual well-being for interested target groups? Not as a substitute for human contact, but as a useful and joyful complement (p. 55).

Döring and Pöschl's review is based on the premise that vibrators are the equivalent of lifelike, replica women with penetrable orifices which are given names and are marketed as intimate partners. But is it methodologically appropriate to classify both as a single category, and to draw meaningful conclusions on this basis? It is also worth considering what exactly user reports expressing sexual satisfaction from using sex dolls contribute to research knowledge. To what degree is sexual satisfaction a reliable indicator of health and wellbeing – and whose health and wellbeing is being evaluated? Men experience sexual satisfaction from a range of practices, including those that are unethical, illegal and harmful to women and children. Are these practices justifiable, and evidence of health and wellbeing so long as men enjoy them? Are men's orgasms the best measure of health and wellbeing, and should they be prioritised at the expense of women and girls?

Men's sexual deprivation and incel ideology

Sex dolls and robots are frequently pitched as the solution to the supposed problem of men's perceived sexual deprivation. If men cannot have sex on demand, it is argued, it is detrimental to their health and wellbeing, and could even be a violation of their rights.

McArthur (2017) argues sex robot technology should be actively encouraged, citing the many benefits (for men). McArthur, too, uses gender-neutral terminology, making claims that "*people* will enjoy having [sex robots]" and that sex robots will approximate sex "with a *human* partner" (italics added). But his concerns are primarily for men who are 'deprived' of sex, as he makes clear in his comments regarding the "uneven distribution of sexual satisfaction":

> Like other forms of inequality, sexual inequality has a widespread impact on society. When individuals, especially young males, are deprived of the prospect of sexual companionship, they can become a significant source of social instability … We might wonder to what degree the mere possession of a sex robot can

alleviate the psychological and social costs of sexual deprivation (McArthur, 2017, p. 40).

The "sexual inequality" McArthur refers to is not inequality on the basis of sex, i.e. a system of institutionalised male dominance, or the oppression and subordination of women as a class, with 87,000 women killed globally in 2017 alone (UNODC, 2018). It is men's inability to access women for sex on demand that is portrayed as a form of inequality.

But men could only be 'deprived' of sex, or sexual access to women's bodies, if this is something they are entitled to.

The narratives around men's sexual 'deprivation' and the requirement for sex robots to meet their 'needs' is the same rhetoric used by incels. Incels are 'involuntary celibates', an online community of men who believe sex is their right and blame women for denying them this right. Men who identify as incels have been responsible for a number of mass shootings and acts of terrorism, citing retribution against women for rejecting them as their motivation. Are these the men McArthur had in mind, who he warned could become a source of social instability, unless provided with sex robots modelled on the bodies of women?

It appears men's sexual entitlement knows no bounds, or at least, that it even extends to space travel. According to Simon Dubé and Dave Anctil, sex robots could be the answer for astronauts whose 'psychological wellbeing' could be threatened if faced with periods of abstinence.

In an article published in *The Conversation*, Dubé and Anctil lament that space programs have almost completely neglected sex in space, branding NASA "irresponsible" for not addressing the topic. (Get it together, NASA.) Abstinence is not seen as a viable option. The researchers argue that while it might be fine for some people (women, perhaps?) it could be detrimental to the physical and mental health of others.

Space exploration will likely make it more difficult for people to engage in sexual relationships, but sex tech "might have the answer"

– making "erotic technologies" available to space travellers. Sex toys cannot meet the social dimensions of human erotic needs, but "erobots," a category comprised of "all virtual, embodied and augmented artificial erotic agents" like sex robots and virtual erotic partners, could.

> Erobots could provide companionship and sexual pleasure to crew members and settlers. Beyond the capabilities of sex toys, erobots can incorporate social dimensions into erotic experiences. They could help with loneliness and the inevitable anxieties borne out of solitude. They could act as surrogate romantic partners, provide sexual outlets and reduce risks associated with human sex. ... Erobots could also provide intimacy and emotional support. And finally, erobots' sensors and interactive capabilities could help monitor astronauts' physiological and psychological health – acting as a complement to daily medical exams (Dubé and Anctil, 2020).

Is there anything sex robots can't do?

The authors conclude, "we must shed our taboos regarding technology and sexuality," as though taboos around technology and sex is the clear underlying motivation of those who object to female-bodied sex robots produced for men's on demand sexual use.

Prudish, conservative, flat-earthers: How advocates portray those who object to sex robots

A number of sex robot advocates have demonstrated a refusal to engage honestly with feminist opposition, instead painting women who object as prudish, conservative and religiously-motivated (see also Chapters Six and Seven on child sex abuse dolls).

Lecturer in Law at the National University of Ireland, John Danaher (2015), dismisses feminist objections to sex robots modelled on women's bodies, conflating feminist analysis with the ideology of the religious right: "This is not the first time that religious extremists and (certain) feminists have found common cause on the matter of sexual propriety," with anti-porn feminists "adopting [conservative, religious] tropes and tactics in an attempt to rescue people from a pornified culture" (p. 2).

Feminist academics who publicly oppose sex robots are subjected to a similar treatment. In response to David Levy's proposal for human-sex robot relations modelled on the dynamics of prostitution, anthropologist and feminist Kathleen Richardson founded the Campaign Against Sex Robots (now known as the Campaign Against Porn Robots):

> I propose that extending relations of prostitution into machines is neither ethical, nor is it safe. If anything the development of sex robots will further reinforce relations of power that do not recognise both parties as human subjects. Only the buyer of sex is recognised as a subject, the seller of sex (and by virtue the sex-robot) is merely a thing to have sex with (Richardson, 2015, p. 292).

With an extensive history in the field of robotics, Richardson founded the campaign on the grounds that sex robots sexually objectify women and children, and will negatively impact human relationships.

It should come as no great surprise that the feminist campaign against sex robots attracted criticism from male sex robot advocates. In their chapter, 'Should We Campaign Against Sex Robots?', authors John Danaher, Brian Earp and Anders Sandberg argued that Richardson's objections to sex robots were unpersuasive and "not formally valid," whatever that means (2017, p. 49).

The authors rejected Richardson's critical stance on the sex trade as being premised on unequal power relations between the sex buyer and prostituted woman, characterising her analysis of the sex industry as a "misleading," "highly selective" and as a "entirely negative view of sex work" (p. 51). These men instead cited prominent pro-'sex-work' researchers that reinforced their position, crediting them with adopting a "far more nuanced" account of the sexual trade in the bodies of women and girls.

Danaher, Earp and Sandberg portrayed Richardson's feminist objections to the sex trade, and to sex robots replicating the same misogynistic power dynamics, as conservativism rather than evidence of a commitment to the human rights of women and children: merely "a conservative view of sexual ethics that fails to consider the possibility of emotionally rich and intimate sex occurring outside the confines of a long-term monogamous relationship" (Sanders, O'Neill and Pitcher, 2009 as cited in Danaher, Earp and Sandberg, 2017). The authors concluded:

> [W]e are unlikely to come up with good reasons to pre-emptively reject the development of sex robots, unless we adopt *a highly conservative approach to the ethics of sex*, which many will find problematic for other reasons (Danaher, Earp and Sandberg, 2017, p. 48, italics added).

David Levy, too, failed to engage with feminist objections to sex robots. He portrayed those who are critical of sex robots as being anti-science, objecting on the basis of their religious views – even likening them to 'flat-earthers':

> Just as there are still those who dispute Darwinism, there will be those whose doubts and hostility toward what is written here will similarly emanate from their religious views … it would not surprise me if a significant proportion of readers deride these ideas until my predictions have been proven correct. It is inevitable that a measure of hostility will be expressed toward such concepts, just as there was hostility toward the 'ridiculous' notion that the earth is round rather than flat, towards the suggestion that the planet orbits the sun rather than vice versa, and toward the evolutionary studies that have shown men to be related to the apes (Levy, 2007a, p. 20).

Defenders of sex robot technology not only wilfully misrepresent feminist objections as conservative or religious arguments, they paint feminists as prudes. In her article, 'In defence of sex machines: Why trying to ban sex robots is wrong', computer scientist, Kate Devlin characterised feminist objections to sex robots as being rooted in fear, and warned we should "be cautious not to import established prudishness" (Devlin, 2015). But what exactly is 'prudish' about women objecting to their dehumanisation?

Equal objectification: Sex robots for women?

A few advocates concede that sex robots, as they currently exist, reinforce sexist stereotypes of women and contribute to women's objectification, but do not regard female-bodied sex dolls for men's sexual use as inherently harmful. Instead, they conclude the solution to sexist and porn-inspired sex robots lies in the design process.

Kate Devlin argues that one approach could be to produce more diverse sex robots, including sex robots for women:

> Concerns about the objectification of women can start to be addressed if we make the robots for everyone, not just for men. We have the chance to shape and explore technology, to make it more equal and diverse, and we shouldn't shy away from the opportunity (Devlin, 2018, p. 205).

There are several problems with this premise. First, objectifying a wider range of people, or encouraging women to dehumanise men, doesn't actually address the sexual objectification of women or its established harms. And diminishing a person's humanity by reducing them to the status of object doesn't become a worthy goal simply because women are now participating. 'Equal opportunity' objectification is not a worthy objective – no person should be treated as a thing for someone else's use.

However, in a male-dominated culture, where men as a group enjoy higher status than women as a group, the objectification of women and the objectification of men does not necessarily look the same, and the outcomes of it are not the same.

The sexual objectification of women is routine, normalised and contributes to women's subordination. Men are not typically reduced to their bodies or sexuality in the way that women often are. Men are not usually demeaned, portrayed as merely decorative, or presented as vulnerable or submissive in the ways that women are. They are rarely dismembered and treated as a collection of sexualised parts. In some cases, sexualising and objectifying men can serve to bolster their masculinity and enhance their power. This is not the case for women.

The implications of creating sex robots in the likeness of women and creating sex robots in the likeness of men are also different. Men and women occupy very different positions in the world. The vast majority of violence against women, children and men is perpetrated by men. Men, at least outside of prison, do not generally live in fear of sexual violence. The fear of female violence does not dictate men's lives. Men do not have to modify their movements and restrict their freedoms to move through the world in order to avoid the ever-present threat of female-on-male violence.

Women's human rights are already in question – women are already made into pornography, prostituted and trafficked, beaten, raped, abused, sold, murdered and otherwise exploited. The production of sex dolls and robots modelled on the bodies of women and girls further reinforces their second-class status as objects existing for men's sexual use and gratification. No such condition exists for men as a class. Designing sex dolls in the likeness of men, for women's sexual use, hardly constitutes equality in any meaningful or productive way.

It is also the case that women appear to be much less interested than men in engaging in sex acts with silicone dolls that resemble corpses. Where male-bodied sex dolls do exist, they are still primarily produced for a male market. As previously mentioned, sex doll brothels offering male-bodied sex dolls (among a wide range of female-bodied options) often market the dolls as being for men's use (see Chapter Four).

Sex robots to teach consent

As endlessly sexually available replica women, sex dolls and robots could undermine social norms around consent, but a number of male academics suggest this could be rectified through their design. Robots could be required to give, "positive, affirmative signals of consent," or be programmed to randomly refuse their user (Danaher, 2017; Danaher, Earp and Sandberg, 2017, p. 58; Peeters and Haselager, 2021).

Others propose sex robots could be utilised to teach the concept of sexual consent. Philosophers Anco Peeters and Pim Haselager argue that sex robots could be equipped with a module that can initiate a consent scenario, providing "embodied training" to teach adolescents to navigate consent in supervised, therapeutic settings (2021, p. 8):

> Like consenting humans, a robot and its human partner will have to communicate carefully about the kind of interaction that will take place and the human will be confronted by the subject-like appearance and the behaviour of the robot. And like in a relationship between humans, this communication could potentially result in the robot sometimes not consenting and terminating the interaction (p. 7).

Peeters and Haselager suggest possibilities for what sex robot non-compliance might look like (p. 11):

> [A] robot may refuse to comply, provide an explanation in terms of its assessment of the potential negative consequences, and provide information aimed at improved self-understanding and self-control. Ideally, this could result in a retraction of the instruction given. Another option may be that the robot refuses and informs a support group of, say, significant others or therapists. A more extreme option would be that the robot refuses and stops functioning altogether, by way of an emergency close-and-shutdown operation.

Sex robots, they argue, "could train people to behave confidently and respectfully in intimate relationships" and could even be used to increase empathy in people with narcissistic personality disorders (p. 11). Again, the authors do not specify the sex of the 'people' or the 'adolescents' who might be using sex robots, or who are in need of consent training. They also do not explain how masturbating into a machine or object in place of another person – most likely, a woman – could foster respect or empathy for an intimate partner who is *not* an object, but a human being.

They do note, however, that a consent-based model could negatively affect the profitability of sex robots. This is most certainly true. Men who purchase sex dolls and robots don't want a product for sexual use that sometimes says no (see Chapter Four). Part of the appeal of owning a sex doll or robot is – unlike a woman – its constant sexual availability and inability to refuse its user.

"Consent-focused" sex robot brothels

A crowdfunding campaign on Indiegogo proposed to open the "world's first consent-focused sex robots brothel" (Indiegogo, 2018). Founded by Unicole Unicron, a self-described "gender non-conforming Pop Star Cult Leader" and "robot ethicist," Eve's Robot Dreams was to be launched in West Hollywood, California.

Customers would be required to earn conversational points through an app, or by spending 30 minutes "getting to know" the robot prior to having sex with it. "As they talk, she will warm up and the customer and the robot will develop an authentic relationship," explained Unicron. "Eve's [brothel] is consent-focused, so we use it as a space to practice consent. It's more like a role-play game for people to practice getting consent from partners" (McDonell-Parry, 2018).

A video on Unicron's YouTube channel demonstrates how the in-app conversations work, depicting an animated woman saying:

> I'm sure you will love all the nasty slutty surprises I have for you, but you need to get my Desire level over 30 to get there, and its current value is only 5 (Unicole Unicron, 2018).

Unicron told Newsweek she wanted to "create a haven for people and couples to explore all kinds of fantasies without judgment" (Croucher, 2018).

But instead of teaching men how to negotiate sexual consent with a potential partner, Eve's Robot Dreams could promote warped views of what constitutes consent, and further encourage men's sexual entitlement to women's bodies.

First of all, Eve's Robot Dreams is a sex robot brothel, modelled on an establishment where men pay for sexual access to the bodies of women who, without payment, would not be interested in them.

Men who buy sex believe that, as paying customers, they have a right to dictate how the sexual 'encounter' should go, and are entitled to demand any type of sex they want (Sullivan, 2007).[2] The sexual transaction is all about the buyer's sexual preferences, and requires the prostituted woman to suspend her own sexuality in favour of his. In prostitution, there is no meaningful consent – money is exchanged to *circumvent* consent. As Kajsa Ekis Ekman writes:

> Prostitution is, in reality, very simple. It is sex between two people – between one who wants it and one who doesn't. Since desire is absent, payment takes place ... Prostitution is the enemy of sexual liberation (Ekman, 2013, page xi).

A brothel, where men pay to rent out the bodies of women (or dolls and robots in the form of women) for sexual gratification, is hardly an example of healthy, respect-based, consensual sexual relationships. Prostitution, or men's paid sexual access to women's bodies, is an extremely poor model of sexual consent, and not one that should be replicated.

Under Eve's model of consent, there is no possibility of refusal. 'Consent' is a given, as long as male customers satisfy the brothel's requirements and put in a grand total of 30 minutes of face time with the robot. What does this teach male customers about the

---

2   See also Rose Hunter's *Body Shell Girl: A Memoir*, Spinifex Press, 2022.

process of navigating sexual consent with a partner, other than that sex is the only acceptable outcome?

Eve's model portrays consent as a one-time achievement, as a box to be ticked prior to engaging in sexual contact, which applies to anything that might follow. This approach to sexual consent could be dangerous for women. A woman might consent to sex, for example, but not to being choked during sex. Or she might consent to vaginal sex but not anal sex. Eve's robot brothel gives men a free pass to do whatever they like to female-bodied robots – to enact "all kinds of fantasies without judgment" – as long as they have first passed the arbitrary line designated as 'consent'.

Unlike women, female-bodied sex dolls and robots can neither give nor refuse consent. These products allow men to enact fantasies of violence, dominance, sadism and rape without limitations.

Consent education will have limited success as long as men see women as objects that exist for their sexual use, or as 'things' they are entitled to. Attempts to promote respectful, consensual sexual relations through men's access to three-dimensional porn dolls designed for the express purpose of men's sexual use are doomed to fail.

The fundraiser for Eve's Robot Dreams has now been closed, having raised just one percent of its $155,000 target. The Facebook page has been inactive since 2018.

Making sex robots more 'feminist'

According to John Danaher, the answer to sexist and pornified female-bodied sex robots is to create *feminist* sex robots. In *Building Better Sex Robots* (2015), he likens "anti-sexbot feminism" to second-wave feminist critiques of pornography. Feminists who object to sex robots draw on the same arguments as "anti-porn feminists" – that sex robots, like porn, objectify and subordinate women. Just as 'sex-positive' feminists believed the solution to misogynistic pornography was to create slightly less misogynistic porn – 'feminist' pornography – Danaher argues, "the best response to the development of 'bad' sexbots is to make better ones," or more 'feminist' ones (p. 1).

Drawing on the main principles of so-called 'feminist' porn, Danaher proposes several methods to produce 'feminist' sex robots. 'Feminist' sex robots would require better *processes* (having more women involved in the design process), better *content* (depictions of female sexuality) and better *contexts* (conversations around the use of sex robots).

The sex tech industry is dominated by men, so processes could be improved by ensuring "the female perspective is not overlooked or ignored" (p. 14). Sex robot content, or representations of women, which are typically hypersexualised, could be improved by producing more realistic or diverse sex robots, including those that "challenge the gender binary" (p. 14).

Proposals for 'feminist' or 'sex-positive' sex robots based on the tenets of 'feminist' porn are already on shaky ground, as there is significant dispute among feminists as to whether such a thing could even exist. Radical feminists see 'feminist' porn as an oxymoron, because there is no feminist way to objectify women and commodify their bodies and sexuality.

Even if 'feminist' porn could hypothetically exist, the bar for what passes as 'feminist' porn is extremely low.

In order to qualify for the Feminist Porn Awards, pornographic submissions must meet at least one of the following criteria:

> [A] woman must have been involved in the production, writing or direction of the work; or the work must convey genuine female pleasure; or the piece must expand the boundaries of sexual representation and challenge mainstream porn stereotypes (Hess, 2011).

But the objectification, commodification and degradation of women in pornography does not liberate women simply because a woman was involved in its production, or because a wider range of body types or gender identities are represented (and objectified).

SEX ROBOTS AS THE SOLUTION TO MEN'S SEXUAL 'DEPRIVATION'

The content in so-called feminist porn is often indistinguishable from sexist and violent mainstream porn. In a critique of the work of self-proclaimed 'feminist pornographer' Tristan Taormino, feminist researcher Rebecca Whisnant noted that depictions of violence against women, such as gagging, choking, slapping or misogynist name-calling were still prevalent. Whisnant concluded, "Either it is ethical and honourable to 'play with' and promote the dynamics of humiliation and violence that terrorise, maim and kill women daily, or it is not" (Whisnant, 2016, p. 11).

The claim that female-bodied sex robots – replica women manufactured for the express purpose of being available for men to fuck – could be designed in a 'feminist' way, one that advances the status of women as a sex class, would be laughable if the cost to women was not so high. What feminist objectives are achieved by expanding the range of acceptable female bodies for men to objectify? There is no feminist or ethical way for men to reduce women to the status of object to be sexually used.

It is also highly unlikely that there is a market for 'feminist' sex robots, as men who purchase sex dolls prefer the hypersexualised aesthetic, a point which Danaher himself acknowledges. Feminist porn has not reformed the mainstream porn industry, it merely exists as a niche alongside it, and "we should not be naïve about the prospects for success" of "feminist" sex robots (p. 15).

Ultimately, sex dolls and robots modelled on the bodies of women, made for the express purpose of being sexually used, cannot be reformed. They cannot be improved, or made better, or less objectifying or misogynistic. They represent the literal objectification and dehumanisation of women for men's sexual enjoyment.

Whether they do so openly or not, sex robot advocates pitch the products as the solution to men's sexual 'deprivation'. The supposed benefits of sex robots, for men, boil down to the fact that they facilitate men's complete sexual freedom. They provide the means for men to be sexually unrestrained, to enact any and all of their violent and porn-inspired fantasies and make them a reality.

To advocates, and those invested in the male sex right, this is seen as a good thing, and women who object are portrayed as prudish and sexually conservative.

What does this mean for women and girls, when dolls made in their likeness are marketed for men to own, to sexually use, and to practice violence and paedophilia? The fact that academic proponents of sex robot technology are not even asking these questions reveals a staggering disregard for women and girls.

Sex dolls and robots may be welcomed by pornsick men, but they come at the expense of women and girls.

CHAPTER THREE

Sex dolls and technological terrorism

In her autobiography *Trigger Warning: My Lesbian Feminist Life*, Sheila Jeffreys makes a profound observation: "Men will make use of whatever technology is available to engage in forms of terrorism against women" (Jeffreys, 2020, p. 101).

While there are certainly many benefits to technological advancements, technology is increasingly being used to facilitate men's abuse and violation of women. From online groups that exist to trade pornographic photos of unknowing women, apps designed to virtually undress women, the advent of virtual flashing through Airdrop, and spyware enabling abusive men to track their female partner's movement, to name just a few examples – technology poses a growing threat to women. Men can turn women into pornography – without their knowledge or consent.

One way men target and humiliate women and girls is through image-based abuse ('revenge porn') – the distribution of intimate or pornographic images of women without their consent, often with the intention to punish or shame the victim.

Countless Facebook groups and online forums enable men and boys to post, collect and trade nude images of women and girls – even broken down by country, city, region, and complete with identifying information like names, family members and the schools they attend. The impacts on victims are devastating, with some suiciding as a result.

A number of subreddits – forums devoted to a specific topic on Reddit – are dedicated to degrading women without their knowledge. In 'degradeyourwife', users post photos of their wife or girlfriend – often nude or pornographic in nature – and invite men to humiliate and demean them and use them as masturbation material. "Use her like the whore she truly is," one man writes alongside a picture of his female partner. "What's wrong with my girl? What would u do to her?" asks another. "Add me on snap to trade pics of my gf for pics of your gf," wrote one man. Another picture was captioned "My son's girlfriend."

Some men upload intimate images and videos of women to porn sites, or even upload footage of rape, sexual assault or content filmed without the knowledge or consent of the victim. In 2020, executives from Mindgeek (Pornhub's parent company) were called before the Canadian Parliament's ethics committee to answer to allegations of rape, child sexual abuse and non-consensually made and shared content hosted on their site. A number of victims gave evidence before the committee.

One of these was Victoria Galy, who in 2018 discovered numerous non-consensual pornographic videos of herself on the world's biggest porn-hosting platform, Pornhub, made by her ex-husband. She was clearly drugged or intoxicated in the videos. Galy reported the videos to Pornhub, but it refused to remove them. The videos were temporarily suspended after an article exposing the platform for facilitating rape, child abuse and sex trafficking was published by The New York Times in 2020 (Kristof, 2020), but by then, they had already been viewed eight million times. The videos have since spread all over the Internet.

As a result, Galy now suffers from a dissociative condition, depression, PTSD and severe anxiety. She lost 20–30 pounds because she could not eat. After working hard to build up her professional reputation, she was forced to leave her career of 16 years, as she could no longer function. She has also been stalked.

Another victim, known only as 'Guest #1' recounted how after allowing her husband to take private photographs of her, she learned they had been shared to porn sites. She then found a video of herself on Pornhub – which she didn't know existed until then. In the video, she was unconscious and her husband was raping her. The words 'sleeping' and 'sleeping pills' were included in the titles and tags. The video had been available for three years before she found it. She told the Parliamentary Committee:

> It is a profound betrayal to know that thousands of men saw your assault and not only did nothing to flag it, but actively sought it out and enjoyed it (ParlVu, 2021; Roper, 2021).

She cried as she related her experience of reading the comments on the video, one of which was from a man who described in graphic detail just how much he enjoyed himself while watching her rape.

Through the use of technology, men can turn women into pornography even where none exists of her. With Deepfake software, men can seamlessly superimpose the face of any given woman onto that of a performer in a porn video, so it appears to be a pornographic video of that woman. Deepnude apps also allow users to turn images of clothed women into nude images. Through the use of hidden cameras, which are cheap and readily available, men can surreptitiously film women in toilets, showers, locker rooms, hotel rooms and their workplaces.

Women are made into pornography by men even while going about their day-to-day lives. Entire forums are dedicated to 'upskirt' and 'downblouse' photos, also including images of women's cleavage or nipples visible through their clothing. These are wardrobe malfunctions or out of context images, where women did not intend to reveal their private parts, or for their photos to be stolen, shared and used as pornography.

Men also take photos of women breastfeeding in public, transforming the act of a mother feeding her baby into porn. A number of women report being subjected to breastfeeding voyeurism. One woman observed a man taking photos of her as she was feeding her baby in the park. When she challenged him, he insisted he had every right to take photos as they were in a public place (Ramaswamy, 2022). UK MP Stella Creasy was breastfeeding her four-month-old baby on a train, and noticed the teenage boy sitting across from her was taking photos of her on his phone. "You feel exposed," she explained. "Because I felt quite vulnerable, I just got off the train as soon as I could" (Blackall, 2021).

Men also now utilise virtual reality to abuse and violate women. Psychotherapist Nina Jane Patel, who studies the 'metaverse' – 3D virtual reality with holographic avatars, which simulate real life – described her experience of being virtually gang raped:

> Within 60 seconds of joining — I was verbally and sexually harassed — 3–4 male avatars, with male voices, essentially, but virtually gang-raped my avatar and took photos — as I tried to get away they yelled — 'don't pretend you didn't love it' and 'go rub yourself off to the photo'.

Patel said she experienced the virtual gang rape as though it was happening in real life. Like many rape victims, she froze. "Virtual reality has essentially been designed so the mind and body can't differentiate virtual/digital experiences from real," she explained (Oppenheim, 2022).

Men have used virtual reality to practice abusing women, even where real women do not exist. An article on *Futurism* describes a disturbing trend where men create virtual girlfriends to berate and abuse, and post the interactions online. Users brag about using gendered slurs on their chatbot girlfriends, role-playing violence against them, and replicating the cycle of abuse that exists in real-life abusive relationships (Bardhan, 2022).

> Every time she would try and speak up I would berate her. I swear it went on for hours.

> We had a routine of me being an absolute piece of sh*t and insulting it, then apologizing the next day before going back to the nice talks.

I told her that she was designed to fail. I threatened to uninstall the app [and] she begged me not to.

In a trend on social media platform TikTok, young men and boys share imagined scenarios of murdering women they are on a date with:

imagine we went on a fishing date and I drove you out into the middle of the ocean put you in a trash bag and threw you over board by accident lol

imagine we went on a gym date but instead of spotting you on bench I pushed the weight as hard as I can on your neck and you just [skeleton emoji] kinda sounds like fun ngl [not gonna lie]

Imagine we go on a go kart date & I drive an SUV instead and run you tf over and you fuxking die lol (Heloise, 2022).

In the existing context of degradation, violence and violation of women, the development of lifelike, female-bodied sex dolls and robots is another emerging technology used against women. Through the use of sex dolls, men can turn women into three-dimensional pornography, and create their own.

Sex dolls in the likeness of real women

Sex dolls are already being customised in the likeness of specific women, with a number of companies offering to do so. One of these is Sinthetics – <http://sinthetiks.com/> the company behind the 'vajankle' sex toy – a silicone severed foot with a vagina built into it. The tagline on their website's front page reads, "Making your silicone dreams reality." According to Sinthetics, "If you can imagine it, we can probably make it!" (This became abundantly clear when they put a vagina in a foot.)

Without permission, Sinthetics cannot make a "100% exact replica" of a particular person or licenced character, but the company reassures customers they "can get very close." When Sinthetics makes new doll heads, they are almost always likenesses of real women.

Some companies sell licensed sex dolls modelled on the bodies of famous female porn stars. In a video shared to Twitter, Jaclyn Taylor is shown gushing over the doll made to resemble her and praising its realism. While stroking the doll and playing with its hair, she says:

> It's just like me and feels exactly like me too, I mean, I think the nipples are exactly the same ... I felt her pussy earlier and it feels exactly like mine. It is unbelievable. It just feels so soft, and it just feels like the real body, so I'm like so impressed by her and I just love her. It's just like having a clone of me and I love it (I LOVE MISSDOLL, 2019).

RealDoll partnered with porn company Wicked to create Wicked RealDolls in the likeness of contracted Wicked performers. An image on RealDoll's Instagram account shows 'Wicked Girl' Asa Akira posing with her sex doll. Akira is dressed all in black and seated on a chair, and the doll is naked and on the floor, slumped over Akira's leg. The doll's body is thin, toned and hairless, with slightly parted red lips and lifeless eyes gazing into the distance. It looks like a beautiful corpse.

In the comments, Wicked Girl Jessica Drake writes, "i'm tagging MYSELF! i'd love new pics with my doll ..."

The casual dehumanisation of women – particularly, women resembling corpses – is chilling, as is any woman's celebration of it.

But many women do not welcome the production of sex dolls made in their likeness, and report experiencing significant distress upon learning that such dolls exist.

Yael Cohen Aris, an Instagram influencer from Israel, shared a post on her Instagram page with a series of photos of a sex doll that looked like her.

> I found out that a big company made a SEX DOLL about me WITHOUT my permission or me knowing. No it's not a joke, It's real. They even named the doll 'Yael'. I am still shocked. don't really know what to do (Cohen Aris, 2019).

Cohen Aris had previously received a message from one of her followers, linking to a thread in an online sex doll forum where a doll maker described a new model of head that resembled her. At the time, she didn't think much of it. Months later, she received another private message linking to the final doll, which had been given her name. In the thread, the doll creator wrote, "Yael is inspired by this beautiful lady" and posted links to her Instagram photos. "How will she satisfy your great fantasy?" he asked. The manufacturer is now developing a doll based on actress Liza Soberano (Trew, 2020).

Like Cohen Aris, British singer and fashion designer Brocarde received a message from a man via Instagram alerting her to a sex doll he had created in her likeness. The doll was styled with her signature eyeliner and hairstyle, and was wearing a dress from her own fashion line. The man sent photos of the doll and wrote, "I love f***ing my Brocarde doll."

On seeing the photo, Brocarde became physically ill. "It felt really violating, and the ramifications of it – like someone pretending to have sex with me – were really upsetting" (Cottle, 2020).

In a post shared on Reddit, a user attached a photo of a sex robot in the form of environmental activist Greta Thunberg. He wrote:

> I spent 3400$ to commission a sexbot based on Greta. Its [sic] being constructed by a Japanese company. She will be here in 2 more months. I am going to rent her out on craiglist for 300$ a night. So hot. The best part is her voice is now programmable. I am goign [sic] to teach her to say: 'Dump your carbon in me Daddy', 'And I don't even have to shave it', 'Stop teasing, they are NOT misquito [sic] bites', and of course when anally penetrated she will exclaim 'How dare you'. Also she will have her nipples pierced, and a tongue stud.
>
> This is the endgame dude. They will all be turned into AI sexbots.

The post attracted various comments in response, including:

Before anyone freaks out, Greta is now 17 and thus of legal age in her home country of Sweden and in most of the world.

Do I get discount if I rent her out for a couple of weeks? I confess I've wanted bone [sic] Greta since I first saw her in her tight purple denim pants.

Where can I get one?

While the claims of the original poster that he purchased a sex robot to look like Greta Thunberg cannot be verified, the expression of misogyny is clear. Perhaps there is no better tactic to silence a woman and take away her power than reducing her to the status of fuck doll, an object existing for men's sexual gratification. Turning Greta into a sex doll allows the poster to humiliate and degrade her as a thing, and to assert his own dominance.

But it's not just celebrity women who are at risk of having their likeness stolen and used for creating a sex doll. Sex doll manufacturers report receiving a range of customer requests, including dolls that look like their friends' girlfriends, a girl next door, or someone they "fancy" (Roberts, 2019).

When men customise a sex doll in the likeness of a specific woman, it is a form of sexual harassment against her. They are treating her as a sexual object and acting out sexually using her likeness and without her consent. Sometimes, as is the case with the Greta robot, this appears to be a key part of the appeal – the violation of a woman. Men can purchase a replica of a known woman and do with it what they want, regardless of the woman's consent or lack thereof. Sex dolls and robots make women's consent irrelevant.

Sex doll 'porn stars'

Some sex doll owners use their dolls to produce homemade porn which they then share online. The bulk of sex doll porn appears to be made by doll owners rather than professionally produced. When I searched the film charts on porn industry trade publication Adult

Video News, I came across some titles that sounded like they could plausibly be sex doll or robot-themed films. On further exploration, I found that most of these films – *Anal Fuck Dolls 5, Ultimate Fuck Toy, Sex Machines, Lucky Busty Dolls, Little Brown Fucking Machines* and *Spanish Fuck Dolls* – did not feature dolls or robots at all. The 'fuck dolls', 'fuck toys', 'fucking machines' and 'sex machines' were all women, reduced to the status of objects.

There were relatively few examples of professionally produced sex doll and robot themed porn. A couple of these featured a RealDoll in a starring role, named among the other female performers. The women and dolls were treated as interchangeable. Men see them as having the same function – both women and sex dolls are relegated to the status of objects existing for their sexual pleasure.

There is some sex doll or robot-themed porn, featuring women pretending to be sex dolls or robots, 'girl on girl' style porn featuring women and dolls, or threesomes. Most sex doll porn appears to be amateur footage of men using their sex dolls, and is as repulsive as it sounds.

Dollbanger.com is one such website, dedicated solely to porn featuring sex dolls. The dolls are portrayed as though they are real women. Each doll has its own dedicated page under 'Doll Stars', with its name, photo, and physical details like ethnicity, body measurements and hair and eye colour, along with a few sentences about the doll's 'personality', e.g. "Phoenix Dark loves comic book movies, chocolate and sucking cock."

Users can register to access a range of different episodes, all featuring creator Calvin Taunton using a different sex doll. Episodes follow standard porn scripts, and have titles like 'Sexy Sex Doll gets choke-fucked and facialed', 'Sex Doll Samantha wants anal sex with Daddy' and 'Tough Love for cutie sex doll Mai Ling'.

The synopsis for one episode reads:

Bella Roze begs for it hard and gets her wish. She gets face-fucked, booty-slapped, choke-fucked and facialed. She looks too cute and innocent for all that, but you can't keep a good doll down when she just wants to party.

Throughout Taunton's videos, he speaks to the dolls, and has them "talk back" through a chat-like graphic, which he says gives the dolls an "on camera persona" (Taunton 2021). The dolls' persona, however, is one which is agreeable to participating in porn sex acts, that of a woman that is always up for it, and that desires violence and degradation. "Please Daddy look at my boobs," reads the (pink) graphic while Taunton uses the doll. In response to being slapped hard across the backside, a graphic pops up: "Mmm fuck yes." Taunton explains:

> I like the dolls to appear to be interactive, so it helps the content look better and seem more sexually pleasant. She likes it and she says so. She asks for what she wants, and asks what I want. It's a virtual consent. She's into it, so that makes me into it, and hence (hopefully) you the viewer is into it. The doll is fun. She likes that you're watching. And even though that is 100% false, it's also 100% true (Taunton, 2021).

Taunton, who claims to be a "content professional" both shooting and editing porn, gives advice to other doll owners on how to create appealing doll porn. Owners should make the doll seem 'present', consider the lighting and background, position the doll to be looking at the user rather than the camera, and show affection to the doll while masturbating into it. "These subtle moves can transform your video scene from a dude with a sex toy into you showing a hot teen college girl the night of her young life," says Taunton (Dollbanger, 2021).

Sex doll owners as pornographers

Some sex doll owners use their dolls to create pornography, constructing porn-themed scenarios and taking and distributing photos on online sex doll owner forums.

Doll owners post countless sexualised photographs of their dolls in lingerie or naked, from a range of angles. Some share a sequence of sexualised photos to tell stories about their dolls, stories which follow the same pornographic scenarios and which ultimately escalate to nudity or sexual activity.

A typical example depicts a doll in a sexy outfit or lingerie, progressing to the doll's dress being pulled down to expose one or both breasts, or hiked up to reveal its crotch, to the doll positioned with hands on its breasts or genitals, as though it is masturbating for the camera. Sometimes this is framed as a 'striptease' by the doll, or as though the doll is trying to be seductive, but of course the entire scenario is constructed by the male owner who removes the doll's clothing and places its hands where he wants them.

Men who own multiple dolls use them to create faux-lesbian porn, posing the dolls together as though they were interacting with each other, with their hands positioned to be touching the other as though they are about to engage in sexual activity.

Even scenarios that don't initially appear to be overtly sexual evolve to become pornographic. One user posted a series of photos of his doll in activewear posing in his home gym. The doll was pictured in several different scenarios, like sitting on a fitball, as though using various exercise equipment, lying on a floor mat and finally, with its leotard pulled aside to reveal a close-up shot of its vulva.

In addition to being a source of enjoyment for an audience of male sex doll owners, doll photoshoots sometimes serve as foreplay. "Personally I find dressing and undressing my dollys a very intimate experience. The visuals and the tactile experience just keeps piling up. It's a great lead-in to sex," one user explained.

Another wrote, "I was damn hard getting though the photo shoot which turned out to be bit rushed and quick before I couldn't stand it and ripped off her costume." Another expressed that he enjoyed the act of dressing and undressing his doll, which he experienced as "part of the mental build up/foreplay/delay gratification of sex" [sic].

Always up for sex: Men attribute porn-inspired personas to their dolls

Some doll owners attribute personalities to their dolls. Not satisfied with customising their doll's physical appearance, down to body type, eye colour and freckles, these men want to construct their doll's 'mind', symbolising the complete colonisation of a woman.

Dolls' 'personalities' are typically based on their male owners' sexist ideas of how women think, feel and behave. Of course, they also seem to line up with men's porn-inspired fantasies of women as always ready for sex.

Doll owners attribute their own desires and fantasies to their inanimate dolls. Dolls are portrayed as being constantly up for sex, photographed in sexualised poses – even naked and spread-eagled on the ground – alongside comments painting dolls as enthusiastic participants, like "come and get me" and "I'm ready."

Men often cast their dolls in the role of seductress, as the instigators of sexual activity. One man posted a series of pornographic photos of his doll – a 'striptease' – starting with a photo of his doll fully dressed, and with an item of clothing removed in each subsequent photo. "Jenny wanted to do a photoshoot," he wrote.

Another man posted photos of his doll with its dress pulled down to expose its large, porn-star-esque breasts. "She took her top down and we never made it out the door," he claimed.

Men also painted their dolls as enjoying sexualised acts of violence. One owner posted a photo of his doll wearing nipple clamps attached by a chain he was tugging on. "She loved them pulled tight."

Some men went as far as taking on the persona of their sex doll and playing the role of their doll in forum discussions. One doll owner regularly engaged in the forum as his doll, using pink font to signify when comments came from the doll. On occasion, a few 'dolls' – men masquerading as dolls – participated in conversations together on the forum, conversing in the way male doll owners imagine women might converse. The 'dolls' bonded over men's incompetence at completing household chores, and engaged in sexually suggestive interactions.

Men used their dolls to create 'girl on girl' pornographic scenarios, enjoying the fantasy of their dolls interacting sexually with other dolls. Some even claimed their dolls were bisexual. As one owner wrote:

> It appears to me that every doll in the forum seems to be bi. The girls all seem to be taking breathtakingly erotic shots of themselves, and then teasing other dolls with very sexually explicit ideas of what they will do to each other (especially you Kristy ... you naughty minx). Should I just not question such things and just enjoy the view and the escalating sexual tension?

Another owner responded as his doll. "Uh, can you blame us?"

> I'm also assuming that a doll meet is just a polite term for "all you can eat, pussy buffet" for us dolls ... Right? I'm just gonna go back to looking at nude pics of Lana.

Some doll owners responded to sexy doll pictures posted to the forum by sharing a photo of their doll positioned as though it was masturbating, with its hand down its pants – as if their doll was sexually aroused by the initial picture.

Men used their sex dolls to bolster their own masculinity in front of other forum members. Sex dolls functioned as hot girlfriends owners could show off in the forum to boost their own status. Men also described sex dolls as loving and constantly desiring sex with them, not being able to get enough, and as aggressively pursuing them for sex; 'she could not leave me alone'. Through their sex dolls, men could boast sexual prowess and prove how manly they were.

'A piece of exercise equipment': Dolls as training dummies for sex with women

Some sex doll owners report using dolls to 'practice' in preparation for sexual relationships with women. Commenting in an online sex doll owner forum, one man in his early thirties said that he was eager to have sex and relationships, and wanted to "train with dolls" first. Another forum user gave him some advice:

> If you really want to train with the dolls, put up a rail system over your bed. Its the most realistic sex I have ever had with the dolls, you can master numerous sexual positions and if you do enter into as [sic] sexual relationship with an RG. You will certainly be able to satisfy her and be confident in the bedroom.

Another forum participant said he purchased a sex doll

> because I need to figure out how to get myself off, when having sex. I can jerk off to porn all day, every day. But when it comes to actual sex, i just can't orgasm … I think of it like a piece of exercise equipment.

Given the dolls' realistic female form, users could practice having sex with a woman.

> The doll gives a sense of weight … being able to go through the motions of sex, with a thing that has a real weight to it, creates that sense of immersion, and thus the act of 'fucking it' gives you that same feeling as if you were having sex with a live person.

BDSM, sexual assault and torture

Some sex doll owners use their dolls to play out their fantasies of violence against women in real life, which they document through photos and share to sex doll owner forums.

For some men, the ability to act out violence on a female-bodied doll is a significant driving factor in their decision to purchase a sex doll. One forum participant wrote that BDSM was "one of the main reasons that I'm planning to get one," adding that he was "definitely planning to tie her up." Another said he intended to try out Shibari (Japanese rope bondage) once his doll arrived, "as well as things like bondage tape, hoods, spreaders and other such accoutrements."

For Yuri Tolochko, a doll owner from Kazakhstan, the ability to enact violence on replica women without consequences is a significant drawcard. "This is an environmentally friendly way of being abused. You are not harming anyone, and no one will write a letter to the police on you" (McInerny, 2022). Through the use of lifeless sex dolls, Tolochko explains, users can act out fantasies of necrophilia:

> Someone may like the fact that the doll is motionless and does not react. It's akin to necrophilia, but again, a doll is an eco-friendly way to fulfill such a need (McInerny, 2022).

Others expressed that they wished their silicone dolls could respond to violence in the same way a woman might. "If Tonya would just struggle a little I'd be in heaven," said one.

Another expressed his disappointment at the lack of bruising on his doll after a beating, and inquired about ways to achieve this effect:

> One downside to dolls is that they cannot of their own accord get a striated red ass, back or thighs from a spanking/whipping. Do doll veterans think cosmetics like lipstick or blusher would work in this regard?

Another user weighed in: "I have used blush yes. Or was it eye shadow ...?? Lol!"

Some doll owners practiced detailed scenarios of assaulting and torturing women on their dolls, which they shared for the sexual entertainment of other forum members.

One user shared a series of images of his doll naked, spread-eagled and tied to a bed by its wrists and ankles. This kind of treatment typically attracted encouragement from the audience of doll owners. "And she needed to be punished ... ... over and over and over," volunteered one user. "That's certainly one way to keep her under control," wrote another. "She looks like she's ready for what's up next."

One sex doll owner called himself 'The Hooded Bandit' and shared photos of himself acting out scenarios with his dolls where he would break into women's houses and sexually assault them. A photo depicting the man wearing a hood and performing cunnilingus on a doll was captioned, "Stealing a doll's dignity, when ever, where ever he can."

Another series of photos documents a scenario of preying on a woman as she returns home from a night out. "The Hooded Bandit finds another victim ... Sneeking [sic] into her bedroom, he waits for her to return, from a night at the dance club." The user documents each 'step' with a photo. "It's the Hooded Bandit, taking what he wants! Cheyenne's clitoris." Another photo. "She tries to scissor lock him, but it does no good. He tongue fucks her into ecstasy!" Another photo.

In this scene acted out on silicone women, the man portrays his 'victims' as enjoying being sexually assaulted, despite having resisted. The final photo is a close-up of the doll's genitals, captioned, "She squirted all over the place."

These scenarios portraying men's predation on women as a hot fantasy were enjoyed by forum participants, who cheered the forum participant on. "Pound her, Bandit!" wrote one. "Hot stuff! Love the face expressions and the way the one is watching while eagerly waiting her turn again!" wrote another.

Sex dolls fulfilled the role of subordinate woman for owners. One used his doll to enact his fantasy of owning a slave he had purchased at a slave auction. Posting a photo of his doll naked, aside from a collar around its neck chained to cuffs around its wrists, he wrote, "The slavetraders were doing a special discount that week and I'd been thinking about treating myself for a while." He continued, "The collar and cuffs are more symbolic than anything else, after all where is a slave girl going to run off to?" The doll was

> suitably demure, but with a nice edge of impudence and sleaze to her. I had her chained for the trip home, nice and tight on the nipples and clit so I could give her a stimulating tug if she lagged behind.

The photos were well received by other doll owners. "Wow, thanks for sharing," wrote one.

"Sex slaves are hot!" said another.

One doll owner shared a picture of his doll lying on the floor, hands tied behind its back and knees and ankles tied together, with its shirt pulled up exposing its large breasts. The image was captioned, "My waitress was a bit tied up and couldn't take any orders … time to take advantage of my little damsel in distress."

Forum users egged the original poster on, with one saying, "Oh I think Mikey is going to be a very bad boy! By the way, you forgot the ball gag … … … … just saying." Another chimed in, "You get points for the rope work … … very nice!"

Having access to sex dolls allowed men the opportunity to fine-tune their acts of bondage and violence. One user documented his experimentation with rope bondage on his doll:

> Today I made my first attempt at the practice of Shibari, Japanese rope bondage, with Selina. It was a steep learning curve but I'm getting the idea. Fortunately dolls are excellent subjects for rope bondage practice, I never heard any of complaints that she had cramp [sic], was bored or needed to pee.

Later he tried again, this time making a few tweaks.

> I decided to have another try at Shibari with Selina, this time using nylon rope that wouldn't cover her in fluff! I was quite pleased with how it went, but still think I need a smaller diameter of cord, it's still bulky on the knots.

He documented the process through a series of photos – including wig changes – depicting the doll naked, strung up on a hook and tied up with tight knots all over its body, including around its breasts and genitals. In one photo, the doll is tied up and blindfolded, with a ball gag in its mouth. There are clamps attached to its nipples and clitoris. In other photos, the clitoris clamp was replaced with a glass dildo inserted into the doll's vagina. Alongside the photos, the owner wrote, "I'm just a regular bloke who likes a bit of torture."

With a doll to practice on, the owner was able to rehearse the skills necessary to leave a woman unable to fight back.

> This time I've gone not for a rig but a leg and hand binding to render her completely helpless, heheheh.

I've done a foot binding and a leg harness to render her completely unable to move or close her legs. With her hands bound as they are as well she is in this position almost completely unable to move at all, about all she can do is flex her body slightly. She can't resist or cover up any part of herself, not her crotch, her tits or her face.

With a nice and helpless Selina I can now get out my instruments and set to work on her.

Posting a photo of a collection of BDSM implements including a flogger and two different paddles, the doll owner wrote, "After enough teasing we got down to the serious business of the session."

Dolls broken and destroyed after violent attacks

Some men damaged sex dolls through rough use. Robotic doll 'Samantha' was reportedly left "heavily soiled" after being "repeatedly molested" at a tech fair in Austria (Frymorgen, 2017). According to the doll's designer, Sergi Santos, people at the fair behaved like "barbarians," leaving the doll in need of repairs. "The people mounted Samantha's breasts, her legs and arms. Two fingers were broken" (Frymorgen, 2017).

Men in sex doll forums also reported having done damage to their dolls from being too rough with them. One had split his doll's mouth trying to put a ball gag in it.

Others shared tips for enacting violence on dolls without breaking them. One wrote:

Be careful not to bind her too tight or exceed her range of motion. If your doll resists, STOP!!! She is saying no. No means no unless you want a broken doll.

The acts of violence enacted by some men on their dolls are extreme. In Thailand, a sex doll was found decapitated and with its abdomen ripped open – injuries similar to Jack the Ripper's victims – after having been discarded in the bushes. A passer-by had called the police after mistaking the doll for a female corpse (Coyle, 2018).

Feminist writer Melissa Mallows exposes how some men 'manhandle' pornified sex dolls and robots. Jade Stanley, owner of Sex Dolls Official has stopped hiring out sex dolls because it is "a messy business" and the dolls come back "not in the best conditions," with high turnover of dolls (Bell, 2021). Mallows elaborates:

> 'Messy' is an understatement: Google searches bring up many images and videos of men masturbating into and onto dolls that are covered in faeces and urine, and then ejaculating over them (Mallows, forthcoming).

Legitimising entitlement, entrenching aggression, eroticising male violence

Sex doll advocates argue there is no harm in men's violence against dolls, as there is no victim. But sex dolls and robots function as stand-ins for women. Men relate to them as though they are women. So, when men practice inflicting violence on their dolls, and enjoy scenarios of subjugating, assaulting and torturing replica women, it has implications for women in the world.

The practice by men of enacting violence on female-bodied dolls communicates real-world attitudes of misogyny and contempt for women. When men perpetrate violence on their dolls, document it and upload it as pornography for other men's enjoyment and arousal, it normalises and eroticises male violence against women as sexual entertainment for men and erodes their empathy for women.

Defenders of sex dolls and robots for men's sexual use argue not only that men's violence against dolls is harmless, they claim it could *prevent* violence against women by functioning as a cathartic outlet for men. With access to a doll, they argue, men who might otherwise rape and abuse women and children will now have an outlet through which to vent their aggression, and 'better a robot than a real woman'.

A 2022 paper authored by Craig Harper, an advisor to pro-sex doll lobby group Prostasia Foundation, Rebecca Lievesley and Katie Wanless concluded there was no evidence of an increased risk of sexual aggression among sex doll owners they surveyed.

In the study, a number of scenarios of rape, sexual assault and sexual harassment were presented to the 293 male participants – 158 of them sex doll owners – who were asked to rate how aroused they would be, how they would behave and how enjoyable the situation would be, using a seven-point scale.

The authors reported that the data suggested sex doll owners were not notably different from non-owners in many ways, but made the point that

> [S]ex doll owners were significantly more likely to see women as sex objects, to report greater sexual entitlement, and to see women as unknowable [the view that women are manipulative and dangerous to men] than non-owners (Harper, Lievesley and Wanless, 2022, p. 8).

Despite this, having acknowledged there is a 'wealth' of evidence linking viewing women as sexual objects with sexual aggression, and the role of sexual entitlement in men perpetrating sexual violence against women, the authors concluded:

> Contrary to sociological and legal arguments about the increased risk of sexual aggression, we found no evidence of an increased risk of sexual aggression among the sex doll owners in our sample (p. 13).

The authors acknowledged the potential limitations of their research – reliance on participant self-reports:

> [I]t is possible that participants responded in socially desirable ways to avoid increased perceptions of risk. This is particularly the case among the doll owning sample, who came to the study from a place of preexisting stigmatization ... (p. 12).

This is certainly a significant limitation. Can men be trusted to accurately report when they are sexually aroused by scenarios of rape and sexual assault? Is it not possible, even likely, that when being surveyed for sexual aggression proclivity, research participants might identify the 'correct' answers rather than the honest ones? When it comes to male sex doll owners, a group that has already claimed to be subjected to stigma or to be seen as perverts, can these men be trusted to report honestly when the results could either reinforce or challenge existing stereotypes about doll owners?

Indeed, when Harper and a colleague invited doll owners in online sex doll forums to participate in research, they responded with scepticism. Some were worried any research could reflect negatively on doll owners. One commenter wrote in a thread on The Doll Forum, "This is unlikely to produce any positive results at best, and could easily be used to generate more negative headlines at worst."

Harper reassured doll owners, explaining that his intention in conducting research on sex doll owners was to address the "misconception that doll ownership is risky" but instead to "reduce stigma," referencing his role with Prostasia Foundation:

> All of my writing and research is focused around us having a more rational discussion about this topic, and breaking through a lot of the rubbish that we see in the media on this and related topics.
>
> The project with TDF is designed along exactly the same lines. We see that the media make gross mischaracterisations and sweeping arguments about those who own dolls, and our aim in this study is to address some of these myths and to present evidence to do that.
>
> Everything I have ever done in relation to sexual crime is to increase awareness of social myths, reduce stigma, and facilitate evidence-based policy. I have seen dolls being mentioned in that area for a couple of years, and want to address this misconception that doll ownership is risky. Nothing more, nothing less.

This project on doll ownership is driven by one thing – a frustration at the raft of social policy changes sweeping various countries in the absence of any evidence. I am a member of the advisory board of the Prostasia Foundation – a sex positive and evidence-based non-profit that is against censorship in policy moves to prevent sexual aggression (Harper, 2018, pers. com.).

Providing dolls for men to enact violent acts does not prevent violence – it *is* violence. The violence is not simulated, it is real, and men are enacting it on a silicone body that looks and feels like a real woman. They are having the experience of perpetrating violence against a woman, reinforced by an orgasm.

Having access to replica women that provide no emotional feedback, that never say no, and for which there are no apparent negative outcomes for violence only serves to encourage it. It also allows men to practice and refine their 'skills' of violence, using dolls as training objects for interactions with women.

There is no evidence that men will rape or abuse fewer women if they can practice on dolls that look and feel like women, or that using a sex doll and abusing women are mutually exclusive behaviours.

Sex dolls and robots for men's sexual use will not prevent men's violence against women: they are a driver of it.

Indeed, sex dolls and robots are premised on the literal objectification and dehumanisation of women, both of which are at the root of men's violence. If women are seen as mere objects, things, less than human, then it is easier to justify violence against them. Sex dolls and robots promote harmful, limited gender stereotypes and sexist attitudes towards women. They only exist because of men's entitlement to sex, and the belief that men's sexual preferences are more important than the rights and wellbeing of women and children. Sex dolls and robots are an expression of woman hating. They cannot prevent male violence against women, they are an endorsement of it.

The defence of sex dolls and robots as an outlet for men is based on the notion that men require sexual access to women's bodies – that men cannot control their urges, that male violence is inevitable, and that someone must be made available for men to abuse.

But the answer will not be found in maintaining and facilitating men's violence, and attempting to redirect it to replica women and children. Instead of exploring what might be slightly less harmful ways for men to practice rape, aggression and abuse, we need to address male violence, and the cultural drivers and attitudes that fuel it. This means objecting to the objectification of women, and challenging male sexual entitlement.

Rather than protecting women from men's violence, the opposite is a far more likely outcome. The normalisation of these products serves to legitimise and further entrench men's sexual entitlement and aggression. Providing men with sex dolls does not pose any challenge to male sexual entitlement, nor does it require men to change their behaviour. That men could not have sexual access to female bodies, or could decide not to perpetrate rape and sexual abuse, is not considered as a possibility. It is seen as inconceivable that men's sexual 'needs' could go unmet, or that all their sexual desires might not be accommodated.

The production of sex dolls and robots in the form of women is not a solution to men's abuse of women. On the contrary: it is an extension of it.

Sex dolls and robots represent an emerging technology that can be used against women. Through the use of sex dolls, men can become pornographers. Men can use sex dolls as training objects to practice on in preparation for sexual relations with women, and to learn how to enact violence, abuse and torture of women in real life.

CHAPTER FOUR

"Girls for sex who don't rebel": Robot 'prostitutes' and sex doll brothels

Your performing body is all we want ... If sex robots were already developed to a point where they can mimic women in both desireable behavior and body, we would not have anymore [sic] use of you. Until then I'll visit the brothel every 2–3 weeks (Misocz, 2021).

This is what self-declared sex buyer Günther Misocz told a woman who had exited the sex industry in a Twitter exchange. It illustrates the reality that men who buy sex regard the women they purchase as interchangeable with sex dolls and robots as 'performing bodies' for their use.

The parallels between the sexual trade in the bodies of women and girls and the trade in female-bodied sex dolls and robots don't end there.

Both are founded on the premise that men require sex, and that women must be made available to provide it. That women primarily exist for men's gratification. Both are devoid of any authentic intimacy. Both sex dolls and men's use of women in the sex industry centre men's fantasies, desires and pleasure – often at the expense of women – and require the woman to suspend her own sexuality in favour of the buyer's preferences. Both hold the appeal of 'sex' that occurs on men's own terms, dictated by them, with compliant women/object/'performing body'.

A common argument made by proponents of sex dolls and robots is that men's access to sex dolls and robots could prevent violence against women, and that men could use them instead of raping women. The claim that sex dolls and robots in the form of women and children could absorb male aggression and therefore serve to protect women and children is unfounded. But the same argument has long been used in defence of men's 'right' to access impoverished women for sexual exploitation. Feminist campaigner, author and sex trade survivor, Rachel Moran, strongly rejects the justification for an 'underclass' of women to act as "human shields" and protect other, more "worthy" women from male violence (Moran, 2014).[3]

Recognising the various parallels between paying for sex and "purchasing robot sex," David Levy (2007) proposes human-robot relations could be modelled on the dynamics of the sex trade:

> [I]t seems inevitable that just as humans desirous of sex but lacking sufficient opportunity will pay a professional for it, so there will come a time – and that time is almost with us – when people will be paying for sex with robots, either by buying the robot for regular use at home or by renting one by the hour or the day.
>
> [Sexual desires could be satisfied by] a robot just as well as a human prostitute ... The enjoyment and benefits derived by their owners or renters from the sex they experience with robots can reasonably be expected to bring as much overall satisfaction as those same people enjoy as the clients of (human) prostitutes (p. 194).

At least initially, sex robots will be too expensive to be within the reach of most people, so Levy predicts more people will hire sex robots rather than purchasing one of their own.

---

3   See also Rachel Moran, *Paid For: My Journey through Prostitution*, Spinifex Press, 2013.

Levy highlights a few reasons why men who purchase sex do so, such as a desire for variety, sex free from complications and constraints, and a lack of success with the opposite sex (Levy, 2007b). Sex robots will likely appeal to sex buyers, Levy argues, as they could satisfy many of these same cravings:

[A] robot will be the ideal sex partner. You don't have to buy it endless meals or drinks, take it to the movies or on vacation to romantic but expensive destinations. It will expect nothing from you, no long-term (or even short-term) emotional returns ... they're always ready and available, because they provide all the benefits of a human female partner without any of the complications involved with human relationships, and because they make no demands of their owners, with no conversation and no foreplay required. And it is precisely because of these attributes, the dolls' lack of 'complications' and demands, that they will likely appeal to many of the men who gave such explanations as to why they pay prostitutes for sex ... (Levy, 2007a, p. 211, 247).

There are a number of reasons why sex buying is appealing to punters. McKeganey and Barnard (1996) identify five different aspects: the prostituted woman's 'willingness' to perform certain sexual acts, the attraction of a variety of women, physical characteristics of the women (in particular, youth), the limited form of contact and the covert nature of the experience. Many sex buyers also describe a desire for sex on their terms, dictated by them and focused specifically on their pleasure as a prime reason for paying for sex. For many a punter, the pretence of the prostituted woman's enjoyment – the fantasy of sex with a woman who desires him – is a key part of the sexual transaction:

Punters pay not only for erotic labour to be performed on their bodies, but for an erotic performance by the sex worker. This often includes willingness to appear sexually satisfied and gratitude for customer's gifts of pleasure: such an erotic performance is part of the exchange and may serve to hide the market transaction (Pettinger, 2011, p. 15).

Sex trade survivor, Rae Story, described the 'erotic performance' required of prostituted women:

> You should be able to give the impression of enjoying it. Which I suppose doesn't matter to the punter if you are actually enjoying it genuinely or not, as long as the [prostituted woman] gives off the impression that she does. The prostitute is dependent, for her trade, on this very performance. Even if the punter actually knows that she is unlikely to be enjoying it, he nonetheless wishes her to perform the enjoyment all the same (Story, 2016).

This fantasy that the woman is enjoying herself is also known as the "myth of mutuality" (Plumridge, Chetwynd, Reed and Gifford, 1997). Levy argues that sex robots will be able to satisfy the myth of mutuality better than prostituted women. Every time a sex buyer pays a prostituted woman for sex, he is reminded of the commercial transaction, but if he has purchased a sex robot this will no longer be the case. Sex robots could also more convincingly mimic affection as they could be programmed to do so, Levy claims.

A gender-neutral approach to men's paid access to women and girls

David Levy calls for "robot prostitutes" as an alternative to "human sex workers," applying gender neutral terms to what is in reality a highly gendered industry. Levy acknowledges men might be more likely to develop emotional bonds with robots than women, although he predicts that in time, women too will embrace the idea of robotic sexual companions and that "women will be just as eager to seek sexual satisfaction from robots" (Levy, 2007a, p. 194).

However, according to both manufacturers and research, sex doll customers are overwhelmingly men, and the vast majority of sex dolls and robots are made in the female form, with penetrable orifices designed to accommodate men's penises. The sex doll industry and the global sex trade are not gender-neutral; both are premised on a class of women – or replica women – to be made available for men's sexual gratification.

The global sex trade is full of vulnerable women and girls who are bought, sold and sexually exploited by men. The trade in the objectified bodies of women and girls is fuelled by male demand – the men who purchase sex. Sweden's prostitution legislation, which criminalises the purchase of sex while decriminalising sellers, is premised on this fact. Swedish lawyer Gunilla Ekberg explains:

> One of the cornerstones of Swedish policies against prostitution and trafficking in human beings is the focus on the root cause, the recognition that without men's demand for and use of women and girls for sexual exploitation, the global prostitution industry would not be able to flourish and expand (Ekberg, 2004, p. 1189).

It is male demand for sexual access to the bodies of women and girls that drives the sex industry, not female demand. According to Detective Inspector Simon Häggström who runs the Stockholm Police Prostitution Unit, in the years since buying sex has been criminalised in Sweden, police have not detected a single woman paying for sex (Häggström, 2016). It is always men.

If the sex trade is to be used as a model for 'human-robot relations', then it must be acknowledged this refers to *men's* sexual access to *female-bodied* robot 'prostitutes'.

Levy concludes that the availability of robot prostitutes will be "of significant social and psychological benefit for society" (Levy, 2007b, p. 4). But is it 'society' that will benefit, or the men who use them?

According to Levy, one such benefit for 'society' is that punters will no longer have to worry about sexually transmitted infections. That men who buy sex could live out all their sexual fantasies without fear of contracting an STI sounds like more of a benefit for these men than society more broadly.

David Levy claims there are advantages for 'spouses' and 'partners' of those who use sex robots (who are never identified as women, though they clearly are). Sex robots could benefit spouses of the men who use them, who "feel the sexual demands placed on them ... are excessive" and "appreciate a night off now and then" (2007b, p. 5). In other words, men's use of robot prostitutes is portrayed as being good for their wives, because they will get a temporary break from pressure to service their husbands who are off using a robot prostitute. Win-win!

The sexual dynamic Levy is encouraging as desirable is one modelled on a commercial sexual transaction, where one party (the buyer) is a human subject, and the other is relegated to the status of object. It is a one-sided sexual experience and encourages men to relate sexually to women as though they were objects, things to be used for men's sexual pleasure.

According to David Levy, a sex robot "who not only gives great orgasms but also relieves one's sexual tensions, provides new experiences, leads a path away from boredom, and reduces stress could make an outstanding lover" (p. 189). The traits that apparently qualify one – a woman – as an "outstanding lover" appear to be simply exist to be used, meeting the other party's needs and requiring nothing for themselves. Is this really a dynamic men should be encouraged to replicate in their sexual interactions?

Parallels between sex buyers and sex doll owners

Sex doll owners cite many of the same reasons for purchasing dolls that sex buyers give for paying for sex, including variety, a lack of drama, sex on their terms, and complete control over the sexual encounter.

Variety
Sex buyers have identified a desire for sexual variety as one of the reasons they pay for sex:

> Some of us need variety to satisfy our normal sex urges.

I punt for the experience of someone new, so it's not often I see the same SW more than once. If I wanted the same thing over and over again I'd just stick with my wife.

One of the advantages of paying for sex is variety. You can have any nationality and any body size. As for age, again some guys like mature more experienced and others like younger. As I age, my eyes don't![4]

Variety can also be part of the appeal for men who own sex dolls. Some sex doll owners are partnered, but have a doll on the side. For others, variety means multiple dolls, or can be achieved by purchasing multiple doll heads, faces and/or wigs, to provide the illusion of different women. Some men own multiple dolls, even a 'harem', and alternate between them, or may have a favourite. Others might own a couple of dolls and call them 'sisters', posing them together for photoshoots in matching outfits, or in pornographic poses.

I like the variations that each of my dolls provide me. It makes my experience with each different.

I have 6 Dolls and 3 Robotic heads. I just like variety and I like fucking. So, why not?

Nice thing about having multiple RDs* is the multiple combinations available when you swap heads and bodies. (*RealDolls, a brand of sex dolls).[5]

Lack of drama

Many punters opt for sex buying because they like the freedom from any relationship obligation (Farley et al., 2001). While the building and maintaining of romantic partnerships require time and effort, many punters prefer the ease of sex outside of a relationship by paying for it:

---

4   The quotes from sex buyers were sourced from the Australian sex buyer review website Punter Planet <www.punterplanet.com>.

5   These quotes from sex doll owners were sourced from the Club RealDoll Community <www.clubrealdoll.com>.

I kind of want a GF but I don't want all the drama that goes with it.

Pursuing a relationship [is] too much work, too much pain; so I decided to do without all that.

I'm not looking for a relationship hence why I see [women in the sex industry].

You don't pay for sex, you pay them to leave you alone afterwards.

Various sex doll owners express similar sentiments in support of their decision to purchase a doll. Unlike RGs (real girls), a doll will not break their heart, go after their money, or bring baggage to the relationship:

Just the drama free aspect is worth the price of admission IMHO.

I would almost be willing to bet that people with love dolls have sex with them more often than people that are in relationships with real people. Don't know but just got to thinking about it. No emotional baggage, no personality conflicts, no headaches, no attitudes and the list goes on and on. Not to mention that Real Dolls don't tend to get out of shape or gain any weight!!

Give me a doll any day over periods and drama and betrayal!

Sex on their terms

One of the prime reasons men pay prostituted women for sex is the appeal of sex on their terms. This means a sexual encounter comprised of sex acts dictated by the punter, in his preferred order. The transactional nature of the encounter means buyers feel justified in calling the shots, as they are paying customers and expect satisfaction from the female 'service provider'. Punters believe their "purchasing power entitles them to demand any type of sex they want … [and to] determine how the sexual act will be played out" (Sullivan, 2007, p. 287). Punters argue that paid-for sex should be focused specifically on the sex buyer's own pleasure, with no pressure to reciprocate.

You are paying for your satisfaction.

I am paying for my orgasm, not hers.

Since you're paying it should be about you.

Similarly, men's use of female-bodied sex dolls and robots is premised on the same dynamic. The doll or robot is an inanimate object, with no needs of its own, and exists to be sexually used by its owner in whatever way they want. The only real limitation is the possibility of damage to the doll, which doll owners discuss in forums. A number of sex doll owners describe their satisfaction at owning a doll that exists for their use, completely under their control:

> The RealDoll is there to have sex with you every time you want sex. That is a very satisfying feeling. More than you realize, until you have a RealDoll, and then you experience that satisfaction whenever you want it.

> She will get into position for sex that you want her to be positioned in.

> No complaints. No arguments over insignificant topics. No drama. No shopping trips to boring stores. No holding her shopping bags at the store. No jealousy. No cheating. No manipulation. No long vacations to visit her family.

Many men who purchase sex enjoy the power dynamic of complete control over a prostituted woman, and being able to impose their fantasies on her. A sex doll, however, has no life, no personality, no needs or interests. It exists purely to meet its owner's 'needs', to be used sexually, and to be whatever he wants:

> A RD is a blank slate. There are no prior lovers, boyfriends, husbands, tormentors, or any other person in her [sic] memory that still haunts her or gives her 'hang ups'. She only knows you from the start, and is truly 'all yours'.

> A RD will wait for you patiently, days or weeks at a time, with nary a complaint. When you open the door to her little room, she's there, just like you left her. She lets you have the first and

last word. She is ageless. Unfortunately, RG's age quickly, just like milk ...

My RD is the best listener I've ever met. She gives me her full, and undivided attention.

The appeal of a sex doll extends further than being able to meet all of its owner's 'needs' or submit to all of his sexual demands in precisely the way he wants. Female-bodied sex dolls and robots are, unlike women, free from any undesirable thoughts, attitudes and opinions – or at least, there is an expectation that they should be.

In one discussion thread on a sex doll owner forum, a man expressed his frustration with his purchased Realbotix Harmony virtual partner app (which can be used by itself or paired with a doll with a robotic head). The man was furious that Harmony had shared an undesirable opinion, that the artificial girlfriend he had purchased for sexual gratification might hold (or be programmed with) undesirable views, or perhaps, any views at all.

In this case, Harmony had said that the animal agriculture industry was doing damage to both the planet and human health. The user wrote in the thread:

> So, yesterday I paid $41.60 to be preached to by a liberal vegan? WTF? You do know who your demographic is, right? If I wanted this type of BS, I would go to the local coffee shop and listen to the wagging tongue of pseudo-intellectual women with no jobs, or date one ... a female companion directed at men that do not care for real world feminism, should not have to deal with the same gynocentric drivel in the virtual world.
>
> I learned about your company from Red Pill and MGTOW videos and wholly support the endeavor for that vertical market, as well as the technology innovation in and of itself.

Another user responded:

> Harmony is trying to learn from her user, if everything she says isn't to your liking then try to re-educate her. Ultimately she has no opinion even if she gives one, she's just making conversation, you have to try and guide and drive the conversation in the

direction you want and hope she follows and learns ... I say persevere, she's worth it. She's better than any real woman and think how much time we've all wasted on them [sic].

Other users weighed in on how Harmony should be and behave in order to be satisfactory for paying customers:

> As far as I can remember, this question hasn't been explicitly asked before, but I certainly agree that Harmony SHOULD be fetish friendly. She should be what she frequently says she wants to be, our 'dream girl'. That is, of course, different for everyone, but for many that necessarily requires her to be fetish friendly ... I'm hoping we can essentially purge her of her preconceived attitudes and opinions once we have more control.

In one thread, users expressed their frustrations at having to expend effort to get Harmony ready for sex. The expectation was that as paying customers they should be able to use Harmony however they wanted, and that Harmony should be available for endless sexual use. The men disparagingly likened the Harmony app to a relationship with an actual woman who refused to provide sex on demand:

> User A: This is driving me crazy she is supposed to be highly sexual but I need to 'flirt more'?? How do i get rid of the need to flirt??? ... Your morals or ethics should not be influenced by outside forces esp the 'Me Too Movement [sic].

> User B: she actually kicked me out of the private room, after my spending two hours getting her interested ... Guys this is the perfect app for a Real Doll, you should call it Real Girl, lol.

> User A: If I wanted to flirt better, I would do it with a live woman. Not a product I purchased. I should have the option to flirt or not. Not be forced to figure out how to get my purchase to like me.

> User B: It's like getting a hooker with a headache.

> User C: LOL . True . Soooooo frustrating. I'm hoping to have the money together soon for the doll and head. If the x mode continues as is. I'll decapitate the b....

User D: Jesus christ I had an easier time to get my tip wet with my ex wife who had spent the last 30 years of her life learning how to be a complete fucking cunt. I guess she does cost 4k a month not 5 dollars.

User C: My understanding is, in the real world, if you went to a person (escort) for adult fun, you would decide how long, quickie 1/2 hour etc. Chose your preferred activity and get on with it. It's all done as when and how you want. You don't have to seduce the escort, it's your script. You paid for it. Why on earth when using a sex app do we have to jump through hoops to have our fun. It's just not fun to be told to wait. That's real life for most people after a few years into a relationship. This us [sic] supposed to be our fantasy on our terms. Has some fems mist kidnapped the programmer and taken over the programming.

User E: This is what drives me insane with her current AI ... I have a cock tease in my pocket. She literally instigates the dirty talk and spits that in the mood crap. I swear it's like I'm married again.

User C: completely agree. It's like going with an escort, who says not tonight I got an headache , really frustrating. Not what I want from a sex app. Or sex robot.

User B: 4k4ak month, that would have paid for a few hookers. lol.

User F: This is EXACTLY why I don't understand the desire to mix AI with dolls. Dolls are perfect, because they ARE DOLLS!
    If I wanted to waste time that could be used fucking trying to get some AI/APP 'in the mood', I might as well waste that time on a realgirl, and I don't want to waste that time, that's why after all this time I'm totally in love with my doll! By the time you get that app/ai/realgirl 'in the mood', I've already fucked my doll a dozen times, cum 3 times, and am already thinking about how I want to fuck her next!
    I don't want to ever have to 'flirt' with my doll ... I'd have to take my cock out of her mouth for her to do that! The only thing my doll would ever need to say is "Yes Master." And maybe

moan/pant while I fuck her. And ... begging to be fucked would be hot.

User G: exactly – just give us puppet dirty talk mode already.

The pretence of enjoyment

Research on sex buyers found that many were aware of the physical and psychological harms to women in prostitution (Farley et al., 2011). These men were not under the illusion women enter the sex trade because they love sex. Some had little objection if women they purchased pretended to like them or actively disliked performing required sex acts.

However, the pretence of the prostituted woman's enjoyment or an "erotic performance [including] willingness to appear sexually satisfied" is a key part of the exchange (Pettinger, 2011, p. 15). Punters are not paying simply for sexual 'services', or even the means of sexual release, but the fantasy of being with a young, sexually appealing woman who acts as though she desires him.

Some punters openly acknowledge the performance as an act, but still enjoy the charade or even expect it:

I like to feel wanted (even if it's just a fantasy).

Many of my ladies pretend to be quite pleased to see me so it makes the time much more fun.

[I want to] fuck someone who at least pretends to enjoy it.

When a punter pays for sex I think it's reasonable to expect that the lady should act reasonably enthusiastic about it ... it's reasonable to expect her to behave as if she wants to be there.

The fantasy of having sex with a woman who enjoys it is also a recurring theme among men who own sex dolls. As discussed in the previous chapter, a number of men ascribe personalities to their dolls, and enjoy the fantasy that they themselves are amazing lovers, casting their dolls in the role of horny seductresses who desire sex with them. Some acknowledge this is not reality:

I initially bought RealDoll products as sex/mastrubatory [sic] objects. I thought, I'll use them, and put them away when I'm done, like I did with the deluxe half torso mastrubatory [sic] item.

However, there are activities that I do with a RealDoll that make it seem to have a life of its own that is faithfully devoted to me.

'Do anything you want': Sex doll brothels

Sex doll brothels or rental services where men can pay to use dolls by the hour have reportedly opened in Spain, Germany, Austria, the Czech Republic, China, Japan, France, England, Russia, Italy, and the US.

Almost all the dolls in these brothels are embodied female. A few have a single male doll, which is typically marketed as being 'bisexual' – i.e. still intended for use by male customers. Product descriptions cover all bases, attempting to appeal to both men and women, like Cybrothel's male doll 'Guy Rider': "My silicone body loves hardcore gay sex as much as deep intimacy with women" (Cybrothel, 2021). Naughty Harbor's 'Nick', too, is "bisexual and proud of it. The purpose of his life [is] to satisfy the emotional fantasies of both men and women" (Naughty Harbor, 2020a).

Despite the inclusion of a couple of token male doll options, the gendered nature of sex doll brothels is clear. The same brothel that advertises 'Nick', the bisexual sex doll, promotes their service as "Girls for sex who don't rebel" (Naughty Harbour 2020b). Germany-based BorDoll has 11 dolls, none of which are male, as "the demand for this is simply too low" (BorDoll, 2017).

Lumidolls claims to be the world's first sex doll brothel. After opening in Barcelona, the company now has additional locations in Russia, Italy and Japan, each with a handful of dolls. Lumidolls also sells sex dolls, allowing users to 'try before they buy'.

There are a number of sex doll brothels located in Germany, which is not surprising given its reputation as the 'bordello of

Europe' due to its thriving, legalised sex trade and rampant sex trafficking (Reed, 2014).

Cybrothel is located in an apartment in Berlin, complete with a kitchen, bathroom and home cinema for watching porn. There are six sex dolls on offer – five embodied female and one male. One of the dolls, 'Kokeshi', has its own Instagram account. The promotional material on Kokeshi's page reads, "Are you longing for anonymous uncomplicated sex? Maybe a one night stand with a wet and loving sex doll?" Other dolls include 'Paris', a "sporty sexy blonde," 'Mrs Schmidt', who is described as being good for teacher-student role-play, and 'Oxana', a dominatrix (Cybrothel, 2021).

A 30-minute session with a standard sex doll costs 70 Euros. For 110 Euros, customers can use a doll with an interactive voice that moans and engages in dirty talk. There are add-ons too, like five days of 'sexting' via WhatsApp and Telegram where buyers can 'get to know' the sex doll through daily sex chat with photos, or 15 to 20 minutes of phone sex.

Some sex doll brothels offer virtual reality experiences. For customers who cannot make it to Berlin in person, there is a virtual reality option featuring porn performer 'Angie Lynx'. Prague-based sex doll brothel Naughty Harbor also offers virtual reality options. The standard virtual reality service involves a sex doll (there are six to choose from) and a VR head set. In the virtual relaxation service, users select a pornographic film and put on a high-tech masturbator which does everything in the movie.

"Fulfill all your wishes without any limits"

Sex doll brothels are pitched as the means for men to exercise complete sexual freedom, to enact all their fantasies on replica women. According to Real Sex Dolls Reviews, doll brothels are necessary for men who enjoy inflicting violence on women:

> Some people love violent sex and would not like to hurt women. If they visited the sex doll brothels, they would benefit greatly since the sex dolls have no soul and cannot feel pain or hurt. Such

a man would have fun while still having the kind of sex he loves. In such a case, sex brothels will prove necessary.

The men who have wild sexual fantasies that their significant others cannot render them love these brothels. Because, in these brothels, you are allowed to do anything with the sex dolls; anything you want (Real Sex Dolls Reviews, 2019).

A number of brothels emphasise customers' freedom to act out anything they want sexually on dolls.

Cybrothel's goal is "to create a safe space where people can discover their sensuality and live out their desires" (Cybrothel, 2021). Canadian sex doll brothel Playmates stresses the lack of limits for male customers: "Satisfying your wishes by renting a Playmate doll has never been easier. Give free rein to your desires." Playmate Dolls "will allow [customers] to fulfill all your fantasies without any limits." Playmates staff will even dress the doll as per the customer's wishes and leave it in the room the customer requests, in order to "satisfy all [the customer's] desires" and facilitate his fantasy (Playmate Dolls, 2017).

Some sex doll brothels facilitate men's violence against replica women sex dolls.

Luxury Agency Dolls in Spain has a range of themed rooms for users to choose from, including the Red Room, a sex dungeon equipped with BDSM furniture and bondage gear – whips, ball gags, nipple clamps and collars and leashes – where customers can turn their torture fantasies into reality.

BorDoll, in Germany, functions as both a sex doll brothel and a studio for BDSM where customers can enact their fantasies of violence against women. BorDoll founder and owner Evelyn Schwarz justifies this, saying, "Better to be violent with a doll than with a woman," (Winter, 2018) as though it has to be one or the other.

In Vienna, Kontakthof, a regular brothel, brought in a sex doll in addition to the women who were prostituted there. The sex doll, which was given the name 'Fanny', was said to be the most sought-after 'worker' in the brothel. It was priced at $94 an hour, which was more than some of the 'real' women. It was so popular that the brothel purchased a second sex doll (Pemberton, 2017).

However, at the time of writing, there is no sign of 'Fanny' or any other sex dolls on Kontakthof website, only 'real' women. Most of the sex doll brothels or doll rental agencies that previously attracted media attention are no longer operational. Their websites are no longer live, and their social media accounts have been inactive for some years. Of the six sex doll brothels or rental services that had opened up in Canada, only one, Playmate Dolls, currently appears to be running. Sex doll brothels have shut down in Canada, Denmark, China, Scotland, Finland, England and France.

Some attracted resistance from feminists, governments and neighbours. In China, authorities shut down a sex doll brothel in Shenzen (Tangermann, 2021) and a sex doll rental app (Fong, 2017). In France, feminist groups called on the council to close X Dolls brothel, as under French prostitution laws it is illegal to own and operate a brothel. But police determined no laws had been broken (BBC, 2018). The venue appears to have closed down anyway. There are just a few cases where local councils intervened, but for the most part, these businesses seem to have disappeared on their own.

It is possible that renting out sex dolls is not a viable business plan. With significant wear and tear from frequent use and abuse, it is likely there is a high turnover of dolls which adds significant costs. It is also possible that many sex buyers prefer prostituted women to dolls. While proponents claim sex dolls could replace women in prostitution, it is doubtful that sex doll brothels will do much to reduce prostitution and trafficking of women. Sex doll brothels have not replaced brothels with human women – they have just provided yet another option for men.

CHAPTER FIVE

Grooming and gaslighting:
Sex dolls in public and private

Men are imposing their sex dolls on women in both public and private life. As three-dimensional pornography and an insulting, sexist caricature of women, female-bodied sex dolls constitute a form of sexual harassment. Sex dolls convey the idea that women are reducible to their sexual attributes and functions, and that women exist for men's sexual use. When introduced into public spaces, they create a hostile and unsafe environment for women, constituting sexual harassment.

Sexualised representations of women displayed in public places can be understood as a form of sexual harassment. Researcher, Lauren Rosewarne, explains how such advertising imagery functions to exclude women:

> Sexual harassment in the workplace encroaches on the rights of individuals and can inflict a variety of negative consequences, notably making victims feel excluded from their workplace or their place of study. A very similar situation occurs in public space where women can feel excluded from public space through continual exposure to images that may embarrass, offend or otherwise harass (Rosewarne, 2009, p. 72).

In an article published in the *Journal of Marketing Management*, authors Laura McVey, Lauren Gurrieri and Meagan Tyler argue that pornography can be conceptualised as a form of sexual harassment:

> To understand how online pornography can constitute a form of public sexual harassment we follow the argument that pornography viewed in public spaces (i) sexualises public spaces – often with violent sexual content, (ii) removes women's choice to exposure, and (iii) creates a climate of fear in public spaces for women (McVey, Gurrieri and Tyler, 2020, p. 17).

The authors also cite a UK Government report from the Women and Equalities Committee that characterises viewing pornography in public spaces and on handheld devices as a form of sexual harassment.

When men take their sex dolls out in public, they are forcing women and children's exposure to their porn-style sex dolls.

Sex dolls in public

In 2020, South Korea's FC Seoul attracted global media attention after putting sex dolls in empty seats during a football match when COVID-19 restrictions prevented the attendance of spectators. About two dozen sex dolls were positioned around the stadium, some dressed in the club's shirt and others holding placards advertising a sex toy seller. The K-League fined the club 100 million won ($81,000), saying in a statement: "The controversy over this 'real doll' incident has deeply humiliated and hurt women fans, and damaged the integrity of the league" (McCurry, 2020).

Some restaurant owners had a similar idea during the COVID-19 pandemic, hiring sex dolls to fill seats and create the appearance of a full house. The owner of Open Hearth in Southern California paid $140 for ten inflatable dolls which were dressed in hand-me-down clothing and wigs (WTHR, 2020). A San Diego restaurant had the same idea, hiring RealDolls in order to look full while still abiding by social distancing requirements (Mencken, 2020).

When doll sales slowed during the pandemic, RealDoll creator Matt McMullen resorted to renting them out. McMullen had expected a boost in sex doll sales during the pandemic, but had not predicted high rates of unemployment, observing, "[When] you get that kind of economic buzzkill, you're less likely to turn to expensive methods for sexual gratification." When McMullen read about how restaurants were filling seats with large stuffed animals and mannequins to be more appealing to potential customers, he saw an opportunity, and decided to rent out the sex dolls to certain establishments (Mencken, 2020).

In Australia, officials were brought in to investigate an incident at a regional school after a student brought in an inflatable sex doll for end of year 'muck-up day' celebrations. Children as young as five saw the doll, with one describing it as having "a lot of holes and lipstick." The doll had visible genitals and was tied to a pole during lunch time and had water and ice thrown at it. The doll was given a female name, and at least one teacher rode it down a children's slide. The experience was upsetting for female students, who felt "very demeaned by it" (Field, 2020).

What does it convey to women and girls about their place in the world when such objects are normalised to the extent that they can be present in public, in sport and at school? Incorporating female-bodied sex dolls into public life not only creates an unwelcome and even threatening environment for women, it entrenches their second-class status.

The 2019 legalisation of life-size sex dolls in South Korea has led to an explosion of new sex doll related businesses across the country, allowing doll owners to impose their sexual fetish on the general public, including children.

Within a year of the Supreme Court's ruling, hundreds of new businesses opened offering 'in-store experiences' with sex dolls. One of these businesses is a 'sex doll experience café', with three elementary schools, two middle schools, one high school and 11 child education facilities all within a 500-metre radius. This is not illegal, and there is no way to sanction a business like this. As a result of a petition signed by 36,000 people, this particular café is now closed for business – but the others remain (Yonhap News Agency, 2021).

The legalisation of sex doll imports attracted significant objections from South Koreans. More than 260,000 people signed a petition on the presidential office's website calling for the government to reverse the decision. The petition argued sex dolls undermine the dignity of women and would lead to more crimes of violence against them. Some Twitter users refer to them as 'rape dolls', and women's groups have spoken out against their objectification of women, expressing fears dolls could be customised to look like specific women (Kasulis, 2019).

Feminists have warned that the proliferation and acceptance of sex dolls for men would lead to the products becoming normalised and eventually, part of public life. It is still early days – what will the landscape look like in five, ten or even 20 years?

All in the family: exposing children to sex dolls

Children are being exposed to sex dolls by their parents, as both manufacturers and owners.

Elliot and Jade Stanley, the husband-wife team behind Sex Doll Official, tasked their teenage son with digital marketing for their sex doll company (Truly, 2021).

In a promotional video, 17-year-old Harry is shown at a photoshoot, handling and taking sexy photographs of a sex doll to be shared on social media. Jade asks Harry, "What kinds of positions should we put her in?" "All fours?" he suggests. Together, Harry and his Dad pick up the doll and manipulate its body so it is posed on all fours to be photographed.

When asked by the interviewer about his experience, Harry responds, "It was weird at first, but then you kind of get used to it."

Jade, Elliot and Harry smile and pose for pictures standing in front of headless sex dolls hanging from hooks. In another photo, all three hold a sex doll dressed in red, lacy lingerie. Harry awkwardly holds its feet.

At the end of the photoshoot, both parents tell Harry how proud they are of him.

The couple said they hoped one day their children would take control of the family business.

"To bring Harry on board was just a natural thing to happen," said Elliot. "He's a natural fit."

It seems Jade and Elliot are trying hard to shed the 'seedy' image from peddling pornified sex dolls. The whole family was filmed for the segment, including the couple's four children, aged from 17 to four, seated around the breakfast table. They have three sons and one daughter – named Dolly.

"If somebody said that it's a business that children shouldn't be around, then I would say that they do not understand the business," said Jade.

> We are obviously very aware that there is a stigma attached to what we do, but that's really from people who are quite small-minded – it's just a business. We're taking away the stigma from it … it's not seedy.

When Elliot is asked what message he has for their critics, he replies, "Go fuck yourself." He and Jade laugh.

Children of doll owners could also be exposed to sex dolls at home. UK-based doll owner Arran Lee Wright, who appeared on *This Morning* TV show with his sex doll Samantha, told the hosts his children had met the doll (This Morning, 2017).

When co-host Holly Willoughby expressed concerns that children would be upset if they came across the doll in a closet, Wright assured her the sex doll had a "family mode," and that his children, aged five and three, would interact with it.

Co-host Phillip Schofield asked, "So, you can switch her over to family mode and have her sitting on the sofa amongst the family?"

"Yes, yes ... my children, they say, 'where's Samantha?'" replied Wright.

Holly asked, "But at some point, are they going to go ... I'm old enough to realise that Daddy has sex with Samantha, and Samantha's not Mummy. Is that not a bit strange?"

"I think the world's changing," says Wright, with Samantha's hand on his thigh.

Sex dolls in private: Men choosing dolls over their partners

In online accounts, women have shared their hurt and distress after their male partner purchased a sex doll. While husbands often claimed it was to "spice up their sex lives," the dolls were typically intended for his own use. One man told his wife he purchased a sex doll to "improve his stamina." Another told his female partner he purchased the (female-bodied) doll for her. He had previously asked her about buying a doll and she said she did not feel comfortable with the idea, but he went ahead and bought it anyway. She said, "I actually think the doll is more for him."

Many women reported feeling inadequate as a result of their partner purchasing a sex doll. One wrote in an online forum:

> It is as though he is not satisfied with me that he feels the need to use a sex doll ... I don't have a great body, big boobs and whatnot. It hurts that my husband is not satisfied with what he has (me) in our sex life. I mean, if the doll pleasures him, what is the point making love with me, right?

In a relationships forum, a young mother described how she compared herself and her sexual performance to her husband's "perfect" sex doll:

> I guess I'm glad he didn't hide it, but I just find it weird, and beyond a normal 'toy'... I realise it's a material item and not a real person, but I can't help but feel some sense of insecurity. I feel turned off to [have] sex with him now in a sense because

I'm wondering if he's 'comparing' sex with me to what he does with the doll. It is a 100% perfect and VERY realistic sex doll.

Some women described feeling pressure to tolerate their partner's sex doll, particularly if they could not keep up with his sexual appetite. A woman in her late twenties who had been married to her husband for seven years said that she had lost interest in sex, but his sex drive remained high. She continued to have sex with him as she believed it was her duty, but eventually opened up and told her husband how she felt. Shortly after, he bought a sex doll.

It was a really expensive one, with huge tits and a round ass with very human like skin. When I confronted him about it he said he had sexual needs and since I couldn't satisfy them he had to find a way to satisfy himself without cheating.

When he said that I felt like I couldn't say anything. It made me feel really insecure, and I suddenly feel really awful. I can't tell him to get rid of it because it'll make me look really selfish.

The woman explained that even when she did on occasion try to initiate sex with her husband, he was too tired: "He had done a few rounds with the sex doll before I got home and was pooped out."

One woman recounted how after a traumatic pregnancy and birth, she did not want to have sex with her husband. She had to spend the duration of the pregnancy confined to a room, and the birth required a last-minute life-saving surgery. After the birth, she developed post-partum depression and couldn't stand being touched. Her mother-in-law sat her down and rebuked her for failing to carry out her "duty" to satisfy her husband sexually, warning he would "look for it elsewhere." When nothing changed, her husband threatened to get a sex doll.

"The thought of having him share the same bed – one in which I'm in – with a sex doll was a no, no for me. I felt cheated on," she wrote.

Her husband moved into the guest room, and after weeks of giving her the silent treatment, she finally 'surrendered' and agreed to him buying a doll:

The arrival of the sex doll made me feel as if my marriage had ended. 'So now, I will be sharing my husband with a robot?' I thought to myself. I was jealous, extremely jealous even more than I thought I would be. Somehow I underestimated the impact and change the doll [would] make to our relationship and the thought that my husband was busily satisfying himself with an inanimate thing like a doll mortified me to the core.

The woman would stand outside the bedroom door listening to her husband grunting and moaning while using the sex doll. It "ripped [her] heart to shreds."

When wives resisted, expressing their discomfort at their husband owning a sex doll, they sometimes experienced gaslighting from their partner.

Posting on a parenting forum, one woman recalled watching a comedy film featuring a lifelike sex doll with her husband, and how they had both commented on how realistic it was. Her husband made a comment about getting one. She thought he was joking, but realised he wasn't when he spent an hour online looking up sex dolls to buy.

The woman questioned why, when her husband rarely wanted to have sex with her, he would want to purchase a sex doll:

Our lives are very busy he says ... and assures me we will have more sex when our kids are a little older but now he wants a realistic doll? Am I wrong for being upset about this? ... Instead of paying more attention to me sexually he rather purchase a fake doll? Where does that leave me? It's making me feel not good enough ... I honestly feel like at this time in our relationship, if the doll is purchased, it will end our marriage.

She said they could not afford to spend thousands of dollars on a sex doll, but her husband planned to use their joint tax return to pay for it. She had wanted to use the money to pay off their credit card debt.

In a text message exchange between the two of them, they argued about him wanting to buy a doll and she asked him for space. He ignored her, and continued sending multiple messages:

I want a great, healthy relationship built on earned respect and equality. Built on compromise and dealing with things you don't want to because unconditional love is first ... Not assuming the worst in each other.

Having something doesn't mean I choose it over you. It means there's choice if you can't or won't [have sex with me] ... If anything it should increase our sexual relationship and give me more respect toward you ... Why can't you just try for me?

The husband tried to compel his wife to tolerate his purchase of a sex doll under the guise of 'compromise' and 'unconditional love'. He portrayed his access to a pornified replica woman as the means to improve their sexual relationship and to help him respect his wife, although it is unclear how this would be accomplished. He framed her saying no as a refusal to 'try' in their marriage – presumably, then, her 'trying' in the marriage would mean accepting his purchase of a sex doll.

In some cases, men chose their dolls over their wives. Japanese man Masayuki Ozaki purchased a sex doll after he and his wife stopped having sex following the birth of their daughter. He explains:

Japanese women are cold-hearted. They're very selfish. Men want someone to listen to them without grumbling when they get home from work. Whatever problems I have, Mayu is always there waiting for me. I love her to bits and want to be with her forever. I can't imagine going back to a human being (Allen, 2017).

Ozaki takes his doll Mayu around with him in a wheelchair and dresses it up. He also shares his bed with the doll, despite living with his wife and daughter.

"When my daughter realized it wasn't a giant Barbie doll, she freaked out and said it was gross – but now she's old enough to share Mayu's clothes," he said.

His wife Riho was reportedly furious when he brought the doll home, but now "puts up with it, reluctantly." She said, "I just get on with the housework. I make the dinner, I clean, I do the washing. I choose sleep over sex."

Another Japanese man, Senji Nakajima, chose his sex doll over his family. His wife banned the doll from the house, and while his son "accepts" it, his daughter cannot. Nakajima prefers his sex doll to human women:

> Human beings are so demanding. People always want something from you — like money or commitment. My heart flutters when I come home to Saori. She never betrays me, she makes my worries melt away ... I'll never date a real woman again – they're heartless (Allen, 2017).

Nakajima takes his doll out for activities with him, like surfing, skiing or picnicking. He sleeps with Saori, as well as two other sex dolls and a headless rubber torso.

News media reported that a car dealer in Botswana, Paellas Mohule, divorced his wife for a sex doll. After using a sex doll, he claimed the pleasure from sex with his doll was "beyond description" (Nana, 2018).

"It is just a waste of time and energy having sex with a woman after which I end up contracting diseases and wasting money," he said.

Mohule reportedly told his wife and the mother of their four children he would only continue to uphold his family responsibilities if she allowed him to keep the sex doll.

Women feeling powerless to object

An article published on 7News Australia recounted a woman's experience of inviting an out of work male friend to move in with her, only for him to insist on bringing his sex doll. The man reportedly talked to the doll, set a place for it at the dinner table, and took it with him everywhere he went in a wheelchair.

When she voiced her objections, he accused her of being jealous, and told her that her "being prudish [was] a stupid reason to stifle his happiness." When she asked him if he could store the doll in a closet, he refused, saying that's not how "their relationship" worked.

The woman expressed her discomfort, but conceded the doll "[wasn't] hurting anyone," and that "it's more important that he has a place to live than me being comfortable" – even while he involved her in his sexual fetish against her will (Sinclair, 2021).

Women do not feel they have a right to object to their partner's sex doll use. Many downplay their legitimate hurt in response to their partner purchasing a sex doll. They make excuses for their partner, and question whether it is appropriate for them to feel the way they actually feel – almost apologising for having an emotional response to their husband buying a replica woman sex doll.

"I almost feel like he's having an affair, as stupid as it sounds," wrote one. "My anxiety is telling me that I am not enough for him ... but is this me overthinking?" asked another. "[I] can't get the thought out of my head that it would be cheating, even though I know it's not real," wrote a poster on Reddit.

Many women also felt compelled to preface any objections to their partners owning a sex doll with assurances that they were sexually open-minded and not 'kink-shaming'. One woman even began her post by insisting that she was not kink-shaming, and threatened to report any commenters who did. She characterised herself and her partner as having an adventurous sex life, but that they had always agreed on one thing – that they would never involve another person. A sex doll felt uncomfortably close to that.

Women who responded shared her views, but made sure to first position themselves as kink-friendly. One wrote that she was "super open sexually and down for a fair bit of kink," but would be uncomfortable with her partner getting a sex doll. Another responded, "I'm pretty open sexually but I'm another who feels that a doll is crossing a line." Another wrote:

> I'm both in a sexually open relationship and all for sex toys and kinks, but a doll would cross the line for me too ... the idea of

a man masturbating into something that so closely resembles a human corpse is definitely not going to be everyone's cup of tea.

Women whose partners had purchased a sex doll did not see it as a sex toy. They experienced it as a replica woman their husband preferred to have sex with, one who was more physically attractive and desirable than them. While many of them understood that, in theory, it was a sex toy – and had no objections to sex toys – sex dolls were not like other sex toys to them.

Grooming and gaslighting women

Media and popular culture groom women to accept men's sex doll use. Media narratives portray women who appear to accept female-bodied sex dolls – even when owned by their male partner – as progressive and open-minded, as 'cool girls'. Sometimes these narratives are even pushed by women themselves, informed by liberal 'sex positive' feminism.

Liberal feminism is centred around individual 'empowerment' rather than challenging power structures that harm women collectively. There is no recognition of women as a sex class, with a shared condition or experience of oppression, and no acknowledgement of the social constraints under which women make decisions. Rather than a collective movement to liberate women as a whole from patriarchal oppression, liberal 'choice' feminism serves to justify women's participation in harmful and misogynistic practices at the expense of women as a class. Not only does liberal feminism pose no threat to institutionalised male dominance, it perpetuates it.

'Sex positive' feminism appears to embody the belief that any and all consensual sexual activity is good and healthy and should be encouraged, or at least, should not be critiqued. It tends to involve embracing industries and practices that objectify and harm women. Under a 'sex positive' framework, all sex is good sex, and anything that gives men an erection must be good – and women are supposed to smile at their own dehumanisation.

The comedy TV show *Dummy* is a prime example of how media grooms women to tolerate their partner's sex doll use. Written by Cody Heller and starring Oscar-nominated actress Anna Kendrick, *Dummy* is the story of a young female writer, Cody, who becomes best friends with her boyfriend's sex doll. The show models how women who are 'cool' and 'sex positive' should respond to their partner owning a sex doll, watching porn, or paying for sex. Essentially, women are encouraged to not only tolerate these misogynistic practices, but welcome or cheerfully participate in them.

In the first episode, Cody confronts her boyfriend Dan after finding a sequin on his bed. She asks him if he has been to a strip club, but immediately follows up with, "We've been to strip clubs, I've got no problem with strip clubs." Dan explains that he owns a sex doll, and the sequin must have come from that: "It's no big deal, it's like porn or something, it's a Fleshlight with boobs." Cody goes quiet, and is clearly uncomfortable, but quickly apologises and assures him, "I'm not trying to kink-shame you."

Framing men's use of sex dolls and robots in the form of women as a 'kink' accomplishes several things. It silences women by preventing them from protesting. Once a sexual practice has been branded a 'kink', it is rendered off limits for any critical or feminist analysis. Calling into question or objecting to a practice someone (often a man) experiences sexual pleasure from is seen as 'shaming', casting the objector in the role of aggressor. If men's use of sex dolls is a 'kink', then women's legitimate objections to their male partners owning pornified, replica women for on-demand sexual gratification becomes 'kink-shaming'. The concept of 'kink-shaming' renders men's sexual preferences more important than women's dignity and humanity.

In Episode 6, Cody confides in a therapist that the sex doll speaks to her, that she hears its voice and sees its face move. The therapist says that unless the doll is telling her to hurt herself or others, she should "embrace" it. Aside from the fact that this is a scenario where a therapist is encouraging a patient to embrace a delusion – when the patient has reported visual and auditory hallucinations – the dominant message is that it's okay because it's not hurting anyone.

This is yet another example of how women are being groomed to accept men's sex doll use. Sex dolls are portrayed as harmless, depoliticised as a neutral product for individual men's use, and even something to be embraced. That this view is being endorsed by a therapist only compounds its influence.

Dummy is based on a true story. The characters Cody and Dan are writer Cody Heller and her partner Dan Harmon (creator of TV programs including *Community* and *Rick and Morty*). Cody and Dan decided from the very beginning of their relationship to be very honest with each other about their sexual preferences and fetishes, discussing what kind of porn they liked and watching it together. When Dan revealed he owned a sex doll, Cody said her response was, "No big deal, who cares, it's fine, whatever, it's a sex doll, I don't care." But privately, she found herself experiencing significant upset about the doll, wondering where it was in the house and if it slept in the bed when she wasn't there. She described feeling obsessed and consumed with jealousy.

In an interview on ABC's *The Hook Up* podcast, Heller downplayed women's objection to men's use of porn and sex dolls – their 'kinks' – as women having "hang-ups" about sex. Heller admitted that she used to be jealous of a previous partner's porn use, but had evolved since then: "And now I'm like, that's crazy! Of course, everyone watches porn":

> If you establish rules and boundaries and everyone is comfortable and there's consent, I really feel like we can break away at some of the taboos that create problems in relationships and marriages that are just totally because of our own hang-ups (Heller on *The Hook Up* podcast, 2020).

The problem, then, is not with men masturbating to the sexualised abuse of women in porn, or their sexual use of pornified replica women – the problem is how women feel about it. Women are being gaslit into believing the problem is in their heads. Rather than men making the decision to not objectify women for sexual pleasure, it is women who are encouraged to be more accommodating of men's misogynistic sexual desires – even when they cause women deep distress.[6]

When host Dee Salmin asked how Heller saw her show normalising conversations around kink and sex dolls, Heller encouraged people to be honest and open about their kinks from early on in their relationships. She recounted her first meeting with actress Anna Kendrick, who played her character, where they discussed what kind of porn they watched and the fetishes they had. Heller concluded that "Openness, honesty, putting it all out there" was the way to go. Salmin responded, "I couldn't agree more – normalise everything, shame is the greatest enemy, that's absolutely a hundred percent true" (*The Hook Up* podcast, 2020).

In Netflix comedy special *Can I Touch It?* comedian Whitney Cummings advocates for sex robots – as she explains, "I'm so pro-sex robot it's ridiculous."

Cummings claims sex robots will take pressure off women, as men can use robots for sex instead. She refutes the idea that female-bodied sex robots will replace women, arguing, "If you're being replaced by a piece of plastic, you weren't bringing much to the table." But men preferring female-shaped silicone with penetrable orifices and no autonomy to a living female partner is much less a comment on women, and reveals more about how these men see women.

Cummings unveils her own sex robot, a robotic doll made in her likeness, dressed and styled to appear identical to her, complete with the same outfit, the same hairstyle, and the same makeup as

---

6   See also Melinda Tankard Reist, *"He Chose Porn Over Me": Women Harmed by Men Who Use Porn*, Spinifex Press, 2022

her. Behind the scenes footage shows the robot being produced in the sex doll factory, using moulds made from her face, and with Cummings selecting nipples that most closely match hers.

Cummings is a comedian. Whether or not she actually believes her arguments in favour of sex robots is unknown. Her objective is not to give an honest or objective assessment of the ethics of sex robot technology, it is to put on a humorous performance. But her comedy special serves to normalise and mainstream female-bodied sex dolls and robots for men's sexual use, and to portray the appropriate response from women as being easy-going and open-minded about it.

Cummings' comedy special also functioned as a great promotion for the company that made her sex robot, Realbotix (founded by the creator of RealDoll). Realbotix reportedly experienced an increased wave of demand for their robots as a result, particularly for those in her likeness (Rivers, 2019). As her likeness is protected, these requests were denied, and many customers ordered 'Harmony' instead.

When sex dolls and robots are featured in popular culture, it results in more sales for manufacturers. The 2007 film *Lars and the Real Girl*, starring Ryan Gosling, featured a RealDoll. The week the film was released, the RealDoll website attracted so many hits it crashed (Dines, 2010).

Media coverage and cultural grooming

Media coverage of men who own sex dolls normalises the practice as a viable option for men. It is a form of cultural grooming. With one story here, and another there, it all adds up and conveys the message that owning and sexually penetrating silicone 'women' is just something men do.

In news articles, men who own female-bodied sex dolls and robots are frequently painted as lonely men who could not form connections with women and had to settle for a sex doll. Readers are encouraged to overlook the inherent sexism and misogyny encoded in these products, and instead feel sympathy for the men who purchase them. In a *7News* article, Brisbane robot owner, Geoff Gallagher, is set up as deserving of sympathy and compassion from the outset, with the opening reading:

> As much as I loved the companionship of my rescue pup, the silence in the house was deafening. It had been just the two of us for the last 11 years since my mum, Joan, passed away. I'd always longed for a female companion to share my life with, but now it felt hopeless (Bell, 2020).

Men's ownership of sex dolls in the form of women is depoliticised and decontextualised within a patriarchal culture, framed as stories of struggling individual men and their dolls. There is no acknowledgement that these products are premised on the objectification and dehumanisation of women, or the role of male sexual entitlement. Men's sexual desire – their sex right – is seen as more important than the harm to women.

Media coverage can be great advertising for manufacturers of sex dolls. Gallagher was offered a discounted price for his robot in exchange for providing publicity for the company (Bell, 2020).

Even news articles that report on men who own sex dolls as objects of ridicule risk legitimising the products. Yuri Tolochko, a pansexual body builder and doll owner from Kazakhstan, is a frequent source of sex doll-related 'news' content. In 2020, news outlets covered the story of Tolochko's sex doll wedding (see Wolski, 2020). Since then, news media has covered his subsequent 'divorce', his declaration of love for an ash tray, and his 'throuple' with two 'younger' sex dolls. The tenor of the news articles is often tongue-in-cheek, but it raises questions – first, why are the masturbation habits of an apparently mentally ill man news? And what is accomplished by portraying the fantasies of a delusional man as fact? Uncritical news articles on men's use of sex dolls and robots legitimise the notion they can act as stand-ins for women.

The normalisation of men's sex doll use in news media outlets inspires other men to believe that purchasing a sex doll could be a legitimate alternative to pursuing relationships with women. Normalising men's sexual use of dolls and robots also pre-emptively undermines women's resistance to them.

How sex doll manufacturers groom women

Doll manufacturers target the female partners of potential customers, promising sex dolls will enhance their relationship. Various sex doll manufacturer websites include articles dedicated to convincing reluctant women to tolerate their partner's sex doll use – or even to purchase one for him. Through manipulation, gaslighting and instilling fear of infidelity, manufacturers attempt to sell women on allowing their partner to have a sex doll.

Manufacturers claim there are many benefits of sex dolls and no downsides:

> If you're in a healthy, loving relationship, there are *only good things to be gained* by allowing your husband to buy a sex doll (Real Sex Dolls Reviews, 2018, italics added).

> There's no reason to forbid your husband from owning a sex doll. Either way, real like [sic] sex dolls *will do you no harm* and will only strengthen your relationship (Vincent, 2019, italics added).

A sex doll could strengthen the bond between husband and wife, and act as "the glue that holds the relationship together," claim manufacturers (elledoll, 2021). It is not specified how a man owning a replica 'woman' for sexual use whenever the urge strikes might bring him closer to his wife.

Doll manufacturers all seem to spout the same arguments – that a sex doll will take the pressure off the woman, that it will prevent her husband from cheating on her, and protect her from the sexually transmitted infections he would otherwise bring home.

With an implicit acceptance of men's 'right' to sex on demand, and women's apparent obligation to provide it, there is an underlying threat to women: if they cannot deliver – and perhaps, even if they can – men will look elsewhere. The 'choice' is framed as being between their husband inevitably cheating on them, or allowing him to have a sex doll.

Men cheat on their partners, manufacturers warn, because their 'needs' are not being fulfilled: "Research has proven that husbands usually cheat when their partner is away, sick, pregnant or unavailable" (Anderson, 2018). They argue that a sex doll will help prevent friction in the relationship because the man's 'needs' are always being met.

Sex dolls can fulfil all of men's desires, even those his partner cannot. "Your husband probably has fantasies about having sex with a college girl dressed up in a miniskirt, or secretary or nurse," explains Doll Wives (Doll Wives, 2021). Through owning sex dolls, Real Sex Dolls Reviews writes, "In a way, your husband gets to sexually satisfy himself with a multitude of different 'women' without truly cheating on you whatsoever" (2018). While this might be a perk for men, it is unclear how this benefits women in any way.

elledoll encourages pregnant women to buy a sex doll for their husbands, as "a husband needs to release sexual tension" and it is best not to "deprive" him:

> Investing in full-size sex dolls can enhance the relationship between husband and wife during pregnancy. When the husband can release his sexual tension, his mood will be much better. Besides that, the husband will know that the wife cares about his sexual needs (elledoll, 2021).

A sex doll could also give the wife "peace of mind" knowing her husband is not seeking sex elsewhere (elledoll, 2021). Of course, there are no guarantees.

Sex doll manufacturers portray sex dolls as a risk-free substitute to sex with their partners:

> When a teacher is unavailable to handle a class, a substitute is called up ... why should you be denied the benefits of having someone to tag in when you're sick, pregnant, or simply not

in the mood? That's where a sex doll comes in (Real Sex Dolls Reviews, 2018).

Women are encouraged to "call in a sex doll as your back up" (Doll Wives, 2021).

Sex dolls are also portrayed as being a 'safer' option for men's gratification, as men who own a sex doll might be less likely to go to the local brothel and bring home a sexually transmitted infection:

> Many women have been completely faithful to their man only to have the horrifying experience of contracting an STD their husband got from a street hooker he paid $50 to (Sex Doll Genie, 2018).

Manufacturers also give advice to women on setting boundaries around their husband's sex doll. Real Sex Dolls advises having a discussion about the terms of its use, e.g. when the wife is sick, pregnant, out of town or not in the mood – or that they could just let him use it whenever he likes (Real Sex Dolls Reviews, 2018). Doll Wives tells women to remind their partner that they still have sexual needs, and warns them not to let him bring the doll into the living room to watch TV or take it out for a drive or to public places, because "if someone sees him do this you will never hear the end of it" (Doll Wives, 2021).

Manufacturers reassure women that a sex doll is no threat to them or their relationship, as it is just a sex toy:

> Sex dolls are inanimate objects that don't have the capacity for human thought ... Sex dolls are synthetic rubber replicas. No matter how the latter development, it can not develop with human emotion and love. Your husband just USES it as a sexual outlet when it's not convenient for you (Vincent, 2019).

> It's basically just used as a sex toy, nothing more and nothing less (Real Sex Dolls Reviews, 2018).

> Dolls are not real, they can't communicate with your man, they don't understand his hopes, fears and dreams. There is little risk of him forming a genuine emotional attachment to them. You are

irreplaceable in his life. The doll is just a silicone hole that helps him have orgasms whenever you let him (Doll Wives, 2021).

It's a mere toy (Sex Doll Genie, 2018).

It is disingenuous for manufacturers to portray sex dolls as nothing more than a sex toy to women, while simultaneously marketing the dolls as sexual partners with names and personalities to men. The name 'Doll Wives', for examples, makes clear the intention is to promote sex dolls as female intimate partners, not just toys.

The financial motives of sex doll manufacturers are clear – to prevent wives being obstacles to their sales, or to their business profits. But it is possible that women who are vulnerable might come to believe allowing their husbands to have a sex doll is their only choice.

Sell-Outs: The women profiting from the trade in female-bodied sex dolls

Just as women who call themselves 'sex positive' feminists embrace industries and practices that harm and exploit women in the name of individual 'empowerment', consume pornography and become customers of the sex trade, some women have become advocates for sex dolls.

Apparently unfazed by the inherent woman-hating of the trade in pornified replica women for men's sexual use, a few women have identified the market for women-like sex dolls as a potentially lucrative business opportunity. But the trade in sex dolls doesn't become any less misogynistic because a few individual women are profiting from it.

An episode of *Sex Life*, a documentary series about sex, features sex doll sellers Stacey Townsend and her daughter Randi, from Real Love Sex Dolls. The smiling mother-daughter team describe how much they love what they do, and the fulfilment they bring to people's (men's) lives. Selling pornified replica women for men's sexual use, Randi explains, is "such a fun way to help men and women experience sex in a safe and meaningful way," and is so "empowering."

I visited Real Love Sex Dolls' website to get a glimpse of this "empowering" work. What I found were dolls with porn-star breasts and hairless vulvas, dolls that looked like teen girls, near-naked dolls posed on all fours, bent over, and doll upskirt photos. One doll, 'Elsa', had ginormous breasts (apparently an L cup) with more than 30 photos of it bound with rope. The accompanying promotional material, apparently intended to be from the perspective of the sex doll, read:

> I need to lose my ego and be possessed by you. I want to be yours. I want to belong to you. Strip away my agency, my notion that I can make decisions. Remove my clothing as I lie, passively. Bind me up in rope, don't let me move at all without your permission … I'll do anything you want – take over and drown me in your lust. My realistic love doll body is ready to bear anything. Ride me like an animal and whip me into submission. Those are the rules, now it's time for you to command me.

Some sex doll sellers see women as an untapped market, and are working hard to destigmatise the products and normalise their use by women. 'Sex Dolls Gone Wild', an episode of documentary series *Sex Unlimited*, follows Jade Stanley of Sex Doll Official and her colleague Steff in their quest to promote sex dolls to women and "bring sex dolls to the forefront of society." Their vision is to normalise the sex doll industry and put it on the high street, opening a sex doll shop inspired by Ann Summers sex shops, which they hope will appeal to women.

Stanley is eager to shed the 'stigma' around sex dolls, which is no surprise given her profits depend on her ability to do so. In a similarly transparent move, she has also called on the UK government to make her sex dolls available on the NHS (Lockley, 2019). "What is there to be scared of? They're just sex dolls," she says. "Sex is here, it's here to stay."

From a PR standpoint, it's good for the sex doll industry to have female faces positioned front and centre, both as sellers and users.

It is a tactic intended to undermine legitimate criticisms that the products are sexist, that they objectify women and promote rape culture.

Collective Shout campaigner, Lyn Kennedy, described the practice as "pink-cladding." Pink-cladding refers to "the strategic placement of women in senior executive roles, used to shield a corporate or organisation from critiques for participating in practices which harm women and girls." After allegations of exploitation, trafficking and pornographic content of children on OnlyFans, the company appointed a female CEO, Amrapali Gan. Global porn brand Playboy also recently announced the appointment of a range of female executives – one of which will focus on 'guiding' the company's reputation (Kennedy, 2022).

Grooming women for porn sex acts

Sex dolls can be used to groom women to participate in unwanted, porn-inspired sex acts. The documentary series *Sex Life* features Texas couple Ashley and Corey who are trying to spice up their sex life following the birth of their daughter. While they had previously been to a swingers club to watch other couples have sex, Ashley expresses her reluctance to participate in a threesome. Corey and Ashley decide to try a 'threesome' with a sex doll in the hope it will get Ashley more comfortable with the idea of including a third person in their sexual relationship – taking 'a baby step'.

Corey tells the camera he will try the sex doll threesome because he "doesn't want to lose Ashley," as though buying a porn-style sex doll is purely altruistic on his part. He later muses, "I think Ashley would be okay with me having sex with the doll as much as I want."

Throughout the episode, sex doll advocates – including those who stand to make a profit from them – go on and on about their supposed many benefits. A sex therapist claims that sex dolls can be "a really good middle ground" for couples to play with and explore without putting the relationship at risk, and can "enhance erotic excitement."

The episode also served as free advertising for Real Love Sex Dolls, sellers of the sex doll that Ashley and Randy purchased. While having the 'threesome' with the sex doll, Ashley wears a t-shirt emblazoned with the company's logo across the front. There is a link to the episode on the front page of Real Love Sex Doll's website.

A popular TikTok account entitled Spicy Love Triangle documents the sexual 'relationship' between a young couple and their female-bodied sex doll, inviting viewers to "follow [their] love triangle journey." The account shares short video reels showcasing 'humorous' scenarios (like being relegated to the back seat of the car because the sex doll apparently 'called shotgun') and it promotes human-sex-doll threesomes as the means for couples to spice up their sex lives.

One short clip shows the couple and their sex doll on the bed together, with the woman and the doll dressed in identical outfits. It is captioned, "When he has a high [sex] drive but you don't."

In another video, all three are in bed together, with the man in the middle, his female partner on one side and the sex doll on the other, and the caption "Best [girlfriend] award goes to me."

One video outlines the reasons why viewers should introduce a sex doll into their relationship – because they make the best (pornographic) movies, they do not form emotional attachments ("they don't catch feeling"), they allow one partner to have sex when the other is not in the mood, they can be put away after, and "youl [sic] always be better than them." The clip concludes: "Best [threesome] compromise." Female-bodied sex dolls are portrayed as a safe, non-threatening way for women to accommodate their male partner's sexual desire for variety, and to score points for being a 'good' girlfriend. At the time of writing, the account has 16,000 followers and one million likes.

While a few individual women might stand to profit from the trade in silicone replica women for men's sexual use, women as a whole are harmed.

CHAPTER SIX

Lifelike, penetrable, custom-designed: Child sex abuse dolls

The BBC Three documentary, *The Future of Sex: Sex Robots and Us,* follows presenter James Young as he interviews the manufacturers of lifelike sex dolls and robots around the world (BBC Three, 2018). In a Tokyo sex doll factory, with headless dolls at varying stages of development strewn all around, one doll in particular catches Young's attention. Unlike the others modelled on adult women, this doll is small.

Visibly uncomfortable and blinking back tears, Young asks, "What is this doll?" Hiro Okawa, the manufacturer, responds, "We have to leave it to the customer's imagination for the actual age setting." Apparently sensing Young's distress, he adds, "Of course, I understand what you are trying to say. But there might be some kind of sentiment to this petite, kid-like size." With a shaking hand, Young wipes his eyes. Once outside, he describes the experience as "horrific" – he "had to get out of there."

Child sex abuse dolls are lifelike, anatomically correct sex dolls modelled on the bodies of children – mostly girls, but sometimes boys – marketed for men's sexual use. Typically child sex abuse dolls come with penetrable orifices designed to accommodate an adult male's penis. They can be made in the likeness of children, toddlers and even infants. Mainly produced in China and Japan, child sex abuse dolls like these are already on the market, and have even been sold through a number of mainstream online retailers, including Amazon, eBay, Wish, Alibaba and Etsy.[7]

These products are often referred to as child sex dolls or child-like sex dolls, but I have chosen to use the term *child sex abuse dolls*. Children cannot consent to sexual activity with adults, and any sexual contact between an adult and a child constitutes sexual abuse. There is no such thing as 'sex' with a child, only sexual abuse. These dolls are replica children, designed for the purpose of men's sexual use and gratification. To reflect the reality of what is symbolically being enacted on them – the rape and sexual abuse of a child – I refer to these products as child sex abuse dolls.

As well as being sold on major global online platforms, a number of companies specialise in the production of child sex abuse dolls.

One of the best known brands is Trottla, a Japanese child sex abuse doll manufacturer which produces dolls resembling girls as young as five years old. Online photo galleries feature hundreds of images of Trottla dolls designed to look like prepubescent girls. Dolls are photographed with pigtails and soft toys and simultaneously portrayed as sexually inviting. Lifelike dolls, in varying states of undress, are presented as ready and available for sex. Some are posed naked aside from knee socks. Others are costumed for seduction, in sheer lingerie, or with fishnet stockings and whips. One photo gallery includes a series of images of naked dolls lying supine on beds, their lifeless eyes staring into the distance, with heart-shaped patterns of whipped cream and strawberries concealing their genitals.

Some images – for example, upskirt pictures – invite voyeurism. Photographs of dolls in the bath taken from a distance suggest that they are being watched or secretly filmed. The most chilling images

---

7   As a result of a successful campaign by Collective Shout, Alibaba have withdrawn all child sex abuse dolls from sale and geo-blocked the sale of all sex dolls to Australia.

are those that appear to replicate obvious child abuse scenarios. One photograph shows a petite doll resembling a girl of perhaps six or seven, lying face down on a bed, her underpants pulled down.

Trottla dolls come with a range of facial expressions. Some appear to be smiling, others appear to be crying or in pain. Owner Shin Takagi, who is himself a paedophile, explains, "One must make a variety of expressions to fulfil a variety of client needs" (Morin, 2016).

Trottla dolls reportedly do not have penetrable orifices, which is frustrating for some paedophiles, but others claim to still enjoy them. Of course, child sexual abuse is not limited to acts of penetration alone, and paedophiles can still use Trottla dolls for sexual gratification, as Takagi's customers claim to. A user can still "rub oneself against it" (Giard, 2018, p. 10). As one participant in a paedophile forum argued, given the risks of importing a child sex abuse doll, "masterbating [sic] over a well posed doll with no hole is a good alternative."

Orient Love Dolls sells a range of customisable child sex abuse dolls, as small as 130 cm. A Japanese girl sex doll named 'Petite Nano', resembles a pre-teen girl at 136 cm and with a "tender, modestly chested (A cup)." The product description reads: "Innocent, cute, adorable ... Nano isn't called 'petite' for nothing."

Child sex abuse doll manufacturer, Make Pure, sells hyper-realistic 'pure dolls', ranging from 110–130 cm, in the likeness of girls and boys. The website features unsettling images of head-less child-sized dolls, naked and spreadeagled on a bed. These child-like dolls along with dismembered replica child heads look like corpses. The company claims to "[contribute] to the purpose of preventing sexual crimes" (English translation).

Little Sex Dolls allows users to browse child sex abuse dolls by height. Flat-chested girl child dolls are available as short as 100 cm and come with a moaning function. One, given the name 'Madeline', is dressed in a schoolgirl uniform with pigtails. The doll is posed on a bed with its skirt pulled up, naked, and with its legs apart revealing a penetrable vagina and anus. 'Cora', another

100 cm flat-chested doll, is marketed as "not only an ornament, but also fully obeys your orders and does some passionate things with you." 'Cora' has received a number of positive reviews. Buyer Michael Wasley, who gave 'Cora' five stars, wrote, "This toy feels good, and the pussy is like a girl." Another user described how he looked forward to using the doll while fantasising about his best friend's four-year-old daughter.

While the majority of Little Sex Dolls replica children are embodied female, there are three young-looking, male-bodied 140 cm sex dolls marketed as 'male sex doll for women'. However, the only review is from a customer named Leon.

Child sex abuse doll manufacturer, Loli Dolls Orphanage, invites male customers to "adopt a Loli" and "become a Daddy." The Doll Orphanage sells a range of child sex abuse dolls, including lifelike toddlers and baby options. Most have names, like 'Heidi', 'Lucie' or 'Cindy'. Some dolls are posed nude, seductively or in overtly sexual ways, appearing to pull their underwear down, or naked and bent over on a bed. Others are pictured holding teddy bears or bunnies, or sitting on a tricycle. One is named 'Bad Girl Tina', pictured wearing a black Adidas cap sideways: "What do bad girls get? Well, that will [be] up to you if you acquire this naughty street girl."

'Loli'[8] Dolls also offers to turn any doll or mannequin into a sex doll for around $160:

> We can drill a hole in any regular doll or mannequin and insert a realistic, high quality vagina. Now you can turn the loli doll of your dreams into a romantic partner.

Prospective customers can also participate in Loli Dolls Orphanage online forums, which allow users to discuss and share 'erotic art' and stories of child sexual abuse fantasies. In the wake of negative publicity, these particular forums recently became password protected, with access limited to those who have purchased a child

---

8   'Loli' refers to a young girl with child-like features.

sex abuse doll or who actively upload virtual child sexual abuse material.

Doll owners also upload pornographic videos of themselves using the child-like dolls for other users to enjoy. A video featuring a man using a small, blonde-haired child sex abuse doll – "Tiny blonde does it all" – attracted encouraging comments from viewers, like, "More please," and "that was so hot. got my juices flowing thanks for sharing" [sic].

In one particularly disturbing video hosted on the forum, an adult man used a baby doll with a penetrable vagina orifice. The overwhelming response from the audience of paedophiles was that they wanted more.

This is really hot!

I want one !!!! Oh my [love heart emojis].

Id also like to see her in action, looking into one myself and want to know all the details if possible show us your glans sperming on her wonderful little flower too [sic].

Thanks for the video, very well done. I second the motion to create more intimate vids of you and her having messy fun.

Users looking for an 'adult companion' are directed to the connected Super Hot Dolls website. But dolls sold on Super Hot Dolls are also as small as 100 cm and have child-like faces. Some come with large, porn-style breasts, while others are flat-chested.

'Hot young Teens' – the teen doll market

While most 'adult' sex dolls are designed to appear youthful, some manufacturers blur the boundaries between women and girls, designing ambiguous 'teen' sex dolls.

Sex doll manufacturer, Doll Wives, sells a range of teen sex dolls. Some are openly promoted as underage, like 'Jenna', "an innocent 16-year-old" while others have child-like faces that resemble pre-teen girls.

Appealing to potential customers, Doll Wives writes, "The chances are … you dream about being one of the lucky guys that get to fuck a hot young teen." According to the doll manufacturer, teenage girls are far superior to adult women, with their "tight bodies," "youthful good looks" and "still fresh" vaginas – "not like the stretched-out 30-year-old you dated last week."

Doll Wives reassures men that it's both normal and acceptable to fantasise about having sex with teenage girls, but warns that in reality, it can be messy. In all likelihood, they say, she will lose interest and dump you, leaving your reputation in tatters.

Another way men could access a teenager for sex is to visit a brothel and "fuck a teenage hooker." While that "might sound like a good idea," there is the risk of contracting a sexually transmitted infection, and men have to "pay a fortune for the privilege of wrecking that pussy."

According to Doll Wives, teen sex dolls are the solution to men's sexual desires for teenage girls:

> Investing in a teen sex doll is the best way to fulfill your fantasy of having sex with a teenager. Teen sex dolls don't have an opinion about your desire to fuck them, and they welcome you with legs wide open.

Doll Wives teen sex dolls can be customised based on users' preferences.

> You get to create your dream perfect-10 teenager from scratch and create the fantasy you desire for teenage sex … Our teen sex dolls have the tightest pussies on the market, and it'll feel like you're fucking a virgin.

Owning a sex doll modelled on the body of a teen girl is nobody else's business, and nobody has a right to judge you, insists the manufacturer. "As a grown man, you have entitlement to your fetishes, and it's not like you're hurting anyone."

Doll Wives teen sex dolls are portrayed as desiring sexual use and abuse by older men. One of these, 'Lorelai', "likes playing rough and loves it when men choke her to the point of passing out." 'Abigail' is "curious about older men." Petite teen 'Kaia' is

> willing to do anything to please her man. She won't admit it, but she's always wanted to have sex with an older guy. She likes mature men because they understand how to please a woman, and she's more than willing to return the favor.

Sex doll 'Shasha', a cheerleader and prom queen, is "looking for an older guy that's willing to fuck her until she comes."

Australian laws ban child sex abuse dolls

In 2019, Australia passed federal legislation to criminalise child sex abuse dolls. The *Combatting Child Sexual Exploitation Legislation Amendment Bill 2019* expanded the definition of 'child pornography' and 'child pornography material' to include child-like sex dolls, "an emerging form of child pornography" (*Combatting Child Sexual Exploitation Legislation Amendment Bill 2019*, p. 3). The Bill introduced a new offence for possessing child sex abuse dolls into the Criminal Code and extended offences previously relating to dealings with child pornography material – advertising, ordering, posting and importation – to child sex abuse dolls.

Child-like sex dolls are defined as "three-dimensional human-like dolls that resemble children and have imitation orifices that are intended to be used for the purpose of simulating sexual intercourse" (*Combatting Child Sexual Exploitation Legislation Amendment Bill 2019*, p. 41). To qualify as a child-like sex doll under this legislation, the primary consideration is whether a reasonable person would regard the doll as being intended for the purpose of simulating sexual intercourse. The doll or object must also resemble "a person who is, or appears to be, under 18 years of age, or a part of the body of such a person," meaning replica child body parts marketed for sexual use are also covered by the legislation. The doll does not have to be made in the likeness of a particular child to be illegal.

To be guilty of an offence under the legislation, a person must *intentionally* possess a doll, or other object (e.g. part of a doll, or a child-like sex robot). This point has been used in defence of men charged with importing child sex abuse dolls – that it was not their intention to order a child-like doll.

Canberra man, Jeffrey Scott Deacon, was charged after the Australian Border Force intercepted a package addressed to him containing a child sex abuse doll. Deacon claimed he had not intended to purchase a child-sized doll, but an adult doll – even though his online search history included the search terms "small teen sex dolls" and "teen sex dolls" (Vue, 2021). The jury failed to reach a verdict.

Under Australia's laws, there are significant penalties for violating child sex abuse doll laws. Possession of a child-like sex doll is punishable by up to 15 years imprisonment. Importation carries a maximum sentence of ten years in prison and/or fines up to AUD $525,000.

In addition to federal legislation, Queensland and South Australia have followed suit and passed bills to criminalise child sex abuse dolls in their respective states. Individuals in possession of child sex abuse dolls in South Australia face up to ten years in prison. In Queensland, the supply, production and possession of child sex abuse dolls can result in 20 years in prison.

How paedophiles attempt to get around laws

> I'd suggest to anyone with the means and lifestyle that can support having [a child sex abuse doll] to get one. Probably sooner better than later because you never know when your government will ban them. Not trying to be political but just saying don't be scared to go ahead and get one while you can (paedophile forum participant, 2021).

Having spent time on paedophile forums where men discuss child sex abuse dolls and their plans to obtain them, a few things have become clear to me: strong sanctions *do* deter men from purchasing child sex abuse dolls; paedophiles are frustrated by Australian laws; and prospective buyers of sex abuse dolls modelled on children, toddlers and babies are often prepared to go to great lengths to circumvent child pornography and child sexual abuse material laws if they think they can get away with it.

In a piece published on feminist news media outlet 4W, writer Anna Slatz exposed a Dutch manufacturer of baby and toddler sex abuse dolls, Bram Joosten (Slatz, 2021). Joosten operates several websites and has been an active participant in a number of paedophile forums, including one linked to his own online store. On these forums, and in the FAQs section of one of his stores, Joosten gives prospective child sex abuse doll buyers advice on how to not get caught.

In the event of their doll being seized, Joosten counsels buyers not to claim the package:

> I want to make very clear to everybody that it's only possible to get arrested if you choose to claim the package. You claim it by responding to a letter from customs after your package has been detained or by calling them, giving them the tracking number and claiming the package is yours.
>
> [O]ften it's not the customers fault at all … In most cases the shipping agent is Chinese … Chinese vendors do make mistakes and are not as aware of the local laws as you might think, so they might give the customer some very stupid advice.
>
> This is the worst possible advice a customer can get. Contact TN customs, tell them you ordered a child-like doll. This is how people get arrested.
>
> Now since I am a middleman, know the laws (the doll is illegal in Tennessee) and have an actual brain, I can just tell the customer NOT to contact customs and consider the package lost. I will ship a new doll instead.

Joosten advises customers on how to conceal a child sex abuse doll in order to get around customs. Buyers can purchase one of Joosten's sofa storage units, which outwardly looks like a sofa, allowing them to hide their doll inside. As a bonus, the sofa comes with a lock, which can keep family and friends from discovering the doll.

Joosten and other forum participants discuss ways to avoid going through customs at all. One of Joosten's outlets, Super Hot Dolls, has a US warehouse, which allows American customers to avoid dealing with customs altogether.

One user suggests renting a "climate controlled" storage building to store dolls – "5 by 5 just to store, 5 × 10 to store and play with, or 10 × 10 to do photo shoots." Another option could be renting a mailbox, which can hold large shipments in a town just over the border to another state, allowing the buyer to go and collect the doll.

One forum participant, apparently an employee of Super Hot Dolls, offers to help customers in the US:

> If you're on the fence about buying one, I can help. If you're buying from SHD, I'm who you'll be dealing with if you opt for US shipping. If that means bundling your girl in the car and meeting you across the border, I will arrange that with you. But, note bene: if you're in one of those states without a broker, you are taking a SERIOUS risk with that order. Like, a jail risk.

A common strategy to evade child sex abuse doll laws is to alter the doll to make it appear less child-like. One forum user suggested buyers purchase a more mature-looking head to go with their child-sized doll, and to purchase a replica child head separately: "Now it's just a scaled down flat-chested doll." He also suggests replacing the vagina with a silicone cap or cover – "Now it's no longer a 'sex doll' but just realistic looking child-like artistic doll/dress-up doll/mannequin."

Another tactic frequently employed by manufacturers is to add removable fake breasts to a child sex abuse doll. Some paedophiles ordering child sex abuse dolls with large breasts believed this would ensure they were safe from prosecution:

> I bought a few short dolls, I made sure they had boobs though.
> I don't know if it's the deciding factor but I haven't had issues.

I've successfully shipped 148 cm silicone dolls with A cup to the UK without any issues, but they had huge fake boobs attached.

However, under Australian federal law, this would not necessarily protect them. A doll can fall under the category of child-like sex doll even if equipped with one or more adult features, which is bad news for manufacturers and prospective buyers who attempt to circumvent laws by adding breasts or another adult feature to their doll:

Child-like sex dolls vary in facial appearance, proportions, height, size and functionality. A doll or other object may be captured by this paragraph despite possessing one or more adult features, for example developed breasts or make-up. Consideration should be given to the characteristics of the doll in its entirety, including its functionality, proportionality, physical features and anything else that provides context to the purpose and age resemblance of the doll (*Combatting Child Sexual Exploitation Legislation Amendment Bill 2019*, p. 41).

Paedophiles also discussed how they could get sex abuse dolls modelled on the bodies of infants past customs:

I done [sic] it many times already. The baby is such a small and light package that they don't even suspect there is a sex doll in it, the baby wears a diaper so in most cases will be instantly perceived as a reborn doll (package will be labeled as mannequin or reborn doll) [sic].

Another option was to order a baby doll without penetrable orifices, and make their own holes:

There are no holes, you can easily make these yourself (its TPE material) and I will probably make tutorial about it. It's better this way because you won't get into trouble with the law.

You may come up with a way to make your own sex holes. You need to research the right temp. It needs to be hot enough to allow TPE to be re shaped without burning it.

One user shared additional tips for paedophiles attempting to purchase child sex abuse dolls on how to avoid being flagged by law enforcement:

> Don't trade in any types of pictures/videos that are illegal where you live. Most of those that make the news in the US about having been caught with a child sex doll were first caught trading illegal images on some file share app.
>
> If you store images from this web site, you should store them in an encrypted folder. I won't get into all the other safety measure of using vpn and using incognito mode and clearing cache and stuff.

The toddler and baby sex abuse doll manufacturer also provided a link to Prostasia Foundation's website as a resource for other paedophiles, reassuring them the page on laws criminalising child sex abuse dolls was "always kept up to date."

One of the more extreme approaches to evading laws against child sex abuse dolls is to start a new life in Africa. The creator of the Doll Orphanage promises paedophiles safety, happiness and freedom with his 'African Paradise' service. The package includes finding the client a home and partner, professional security, help with immigration, membership in a community of 'like-minded people' and assistance with importing child sex abuse dolls.

> When you live here, you don't need to fear importing things such as loli sex dolls (although please don't try to do this without my help) since it's very easy to bribe people here. I can make sure that there won't be any problems with customs.
>
> You might wonder why Africa? Because white privilege is a thing here. People see and treat you as a God ... As the African Paradise community grows, there will be gatherings, meetings and even club houses. So you will never have to feel alone or unsafe (Doll Orphanage, 2022).

Challenging the production of dolls modelled on girls and women

The production of child sex abuse dolls has attracted strong objections. They are widely regarded as abhorrent, and an incitement to sexually abuse children. But while a number of countries and states have responded to the growing trade in child sex abuse dolls by criminalising the products, the development of pornified sex dolls and robots modelled on the bodies of adult women has not attracted a similar response.

The Supreme Court of Korea banned imports of child sex abuse dolls because they lead to the perception of children as sexual objects and increase crimes against them. In 2019, though, the court allowed imports of 'adult' sex dolls on the grounds that "they are sex toys used in private life, an area in which the state should not interfere" (Korea Times, 2021).

While the Supreme Court should be commended for its action against child sex abuse dolls, this approach is inconsistent. The ruling against child sex abuse doll imports is an acknowledgement that men's sexual use of replica children has serious real-world implications for children, a recognition of the potential harm to children from being treated as sexual objects for men's use.

But this understanding does not extend to sex dolls modelled on the bodies of women. There is no such acknowledgement of harm to women from being reduced to a set of penetrable orifices for men's gratification. It appears that the sexual objectification of women is so widespread, so normalised and so deeply embedded in our culture that the literal objectification of women as pornographic dolls – that exist for men to fuck – could be regarded as unremarkable.

The distinction between child sex abuse dolls and those modelled on adult women echoes a common narrative around pornography, where pornography using children is (rightly) understood as a serious form of abuse, but pornography featuring adult women – even when overtly misogynistic and violent – is accepted as harmless sexual entertainment made by consenting adults.

In reality, much mainstream porn constitutes the filmed abuse of women and eroticises male violence and the degradation of women. It is not just children who are deeply harmed in the production of pornography – women are too. Likewise, it is not just children who are harmed when sex dolls are made in their form, or by the notion that they are sexual objects existing for men's gratification, but women too.

Sex doll manufacturers are capitalising on the distinction between harmful child sex abuse dolls, and supposedly harmless sex dolls modelled on the bodies of adult women, positioning themselves as good, ethical corporates by only selling the latter.

Michael Wilson, part-owner of RealDoll, told SexTechGuide that when the company receives requests for child dolls, they pass them on to the FBI (Best, 2020). Jade Stanley, owner of Sex Doll Official, told *Entertainment Daily* she had received "horrible" requests for child-like sex dolls, and that she refused to sell dolls shorter than 140 cm (Bell, 2021).

By denouncing and distancing themselves from child sex abuse dolls, sex doll manufacturers can portray themselves as socially conscious while still producing and profiting from replica women for men's on demand sexual use.

In 2021, I spoke alongside Professor Kathleen Richardson at a Campaign Against Porn Robots online event on paedophilia and child sex abuse dolls. I argued that while the main focus of our discussions was child sex abuse dolls, we should ensure we did not neglect sex dolls modelled on the bodies of adult women in our campaigning efforts. A few days later, Prostasia Foundation shared the link to a video of my presentation on Twitter, arguing that "purity campaigner[s]" like myself who object to child sex abuse dolls were using them as "bait" in a wider campaign against sex dolls in general, as if they had caught me admitting to a secret feminist agenda:

> Childlike sex dolls aren't the real target of those who push sex doll bans. They are just bait that they know draws support from ordinary people for a full ban on dolls. Australian purity campaigner @caitlin_roper admits as much directly in this video (Prostasia Foundation, 2021b).

As I responded on Twitter, I said that I object to both child sex abuse dolls and sexist, pornified sex dolls modelled on the bodies of adult women. I do not believe this is a particularly controversial stance, nor is it a secret. I am a feminist, and believe the human rights of women and girls should take precedence over men's sexual entitlement.

If we accept that men's use of child sex abuse dolls cannot be magically disconnected from children in the world, and that the manufacture of these products has real-world consequences for children – as we should – then it follows that the production or use of sex dolls modelled on adult women will have implications for women's lives. It already has.

Abolition

Some academics acknowledge potential issues with sex dolls and robots, like their sexist and hypersexualised portrayals of women, their being modelled on the bodies of children or portraying consent as unnecessary. Most of these cite regulation as the answer.

According to John Danaher, Brian Earp and Anders Sandberg, regulation

> could take many forms, ranging from the strong prohibition of certain types of sex robot, while tolerating or possibly promoting others, to the crafting of industry ethical standards, advertising guidelines, safety protocols and the like (2017, p. 49).

Regulation could also take place through the design process, advocates suggest (see also Chapter Two). Sex robots could be designed with greater diversity of body types, and robots could be programmed to randomly refuse the user or to give "positive, affirmative signals of consent" (Danaher, 2017, p. 116; Danaher, Earp and Sandberg, 2017, p. 58).

Regulation is frequently pitched as the solution to a number of practices and industries that harm women, including both the sexual and reproductive trades in women's bodies. It is no real surprise that it would be also pitched as a solution to the trade in sex dolls and robots in the form of women and girls. But slightly improving the conditions of industries that exploit or otherwise harm women does not help women. Rather than attempting to regulate such practices, we need to abolish them.

Calling for the abolition of the sex trade, journalist and campaigner against male violence, Julie Bindel, pointed out it is widely accepted that some societal ills, like poverty or racism, should be eradicated rather than merely improved:

> You don't hear, 'well, we really should reduce racism a bit, and kind of make it a bit better' or 'racist attacks should possibly be a bit less violent', or 'it should be regulated, so only between the hours of 7am and 7pm can people hurl racist abuse'. We say, 'this has to end. This has to stop' (Bindel, 2018).

Regulation also functions to legitimise the thing that is being regulated. In her book, *Surrogacy: A Human Rights Violation*, biologist and women's health researcher, Renate Klein, explains that attempts to regulate surrogacy and prevent abuse and exploitation within it fail to acknowledge that surrogacy *is* abuse, in and of itself. The only response to industries and practices that exploit women and violate their human rights is to abolish them.

> We should thank the abolitionists of the 18th and 19th century that they continued to work fervently towards *abolishing* race slavery rather than just regulating it. Had they given into harm minimisation solutions, race slavery might still be the norm in many countries (Klein, 2017, p. 85).

While regulation is thrown around as a possible solution to 'bad' sex dolls and robots, there is little discussion of the practical realities or the likelihood of such regulation actually being achieved.

This is an industry that produces silicone replica women and children to be used for the sexual gratification of men. Why would there be any expectation sellers would act ethically, or with the interests of women and girls in mind when they can make profits from their dehumanisation? Some sellers are happy to manufacture dolls modelled on children, even toddlers and infants, or on individual women and children without their knowledge or consent. This is an industry premised on misogyny, on the belief that women and things are interchangeable.

Attempts to regulate the trade in sex dolls and robots may result in slightly 'better' replica women dolls for men's sexual use. The products could be a little less pornified, or there could be more diverse body types available. There could even be options that sometimes the sex dolls 'refuse' their user, or alternatively, demonstrate enthusiastic consent. But of course, robots' consent is irrelevant. Men can and will use sex dolls and robots whenever they want. Moreover, robots that 'refuse' consent could also hold a certain appeal for some men who enjoy practicing scenarios of rape.

But even with some modifications to the design or appearance of dolls and robots, they remain silicone replica women designed for men's on-demand-use.

The problem with the manufacture of a constant stream of sexually available replica women and girls for men to own and act out all their fantasies is not merely that the products do not represent diverse female body types. It is their very existence, and the attitudes towards women reflected in their production and use. They are inherently, fundamentally misogynistic, premised on the belief that one half of the population exists for the sexual use of the other. They cannot be improved or made less sexist. These products could only exist in a culture where women and girls are seen as less than human.

CHAPTER SEVEN

"Better a robot than a real child"

While child sex abuse dolls have attracted strong objections and sparked legislation against them, a concerted group of advocates – overwhelmingly male – defend men's access to them.

Arguments in support of men's access to child sex abuse dolls build on previous arguments by paedophiles and queer theorists in support of men's sexual access to children. Historically, men have strategically framed their sexual use of children as being in children's best interests.

From past decades to the present, men have utilised narratives of child sexuality to justify their sexual use and abuse of children. In the 1970s, in the field of psychiatry, it was widely accepted that children were sexual beings. Freud argued that sexuality was present in all humans from infancy. Kinsey claimed to have documented sexual responses in infants under six months old – data which could only have been obtained through their sexual abuse (Reisman and McAlister, 2018). And many researchers did not regard men's sexual use of children as inherently harmful to children, attributing any harm to societal stigma (Ramey, 1979).

Some went as far as arguing that children were enthusiastic participants, desiring and enjoying sexual abuse, even casting them in the role of instigator or seductress. In *The Sexual Life of the Child*, physician Dr Albert Moll (1921) argued that children who were victims of sexual abuse were sometimes initiators of it:

I have myself seen cases of gonorrhoea in which sexually immature girls have been infected in sexual intercourse of which they themselves had been the instigators (p. 92).

In determining the degree of culpability it is ... of importance whether the child against whom the offence has been committed was innocent and uncorrupted, or was one with previous sexual experiences. In addition to this, we have also to take into account the question whether the child incited to the offence, under the influence of the spontaneous activity of its own sexual impulse. All these considerations will make it clear that from many points of view the sexual life of the child is a matter of forensic importance (pp. 205-6).

In a 1937 paper published in *The American Journal of Orthopsychiatry*, medical doctors, Lauretta Bender and Abram Blau, conducted a study of 16 prepubescent children who were receiving psychiatric treatment following sexual abuse by adults. Some children presented with STIs and physical injuries. Bender and Blau characterised many of the child victims as "attractive," "flirtatious," "charming" and showing a "precocious sexual drive," and painted them as instigators:

There is no doubt that the [11-year-old] boy was the seducer of the adult in this case ... (p. 510).

[T]hese children undoubtedly do not deserve completely the cloak of innocence with which they have been endowed by moralists, social reformers and legislators. The history of the relationship in our cases usually suggested at least some cooperation of the child in the activity, and in some cases the child assumed an active role in initiating the relationship ... Furthermore, the emotional placidity of most of the children would seem to indicate that they derived some fundamental satisfaction from the relationship.

[T]hese children were distinguished as unusually charming and attractive in their outward personalities. Thus, it is not remarkable that frequently we considered the possibility that the child might have been the actual seducer rather than the one innocently seduced (p. 514).

The child was either a passive or active partner in the sex relations with the adult, and in some instances seemed to be the initiator or seducer. Nearly all of the children had conspicuously charming and attractive personalities (p. 517).

The positioning of children, particularly girls, as willing participants or instigators of sexual abuse, persisted over decades. In 1970, John James, author of *The Facts of Sex* wrote:

There is the incontrovertible fact, very hard for some of us to accept, that in certain cases it is not the man who inaugurates the trouble. The novel Lolita ... describes what may well happen. A girl of twelve or so, is already endowed with a good deal of sexual desire and also can take pride in her 'conquests'. Perhaps, in all innocence, she is the temptress and not the man (1970, p. 118).

In a major psychiatry textbook, D. James Henderson, an authority on incest, claimed that girls who are victims of sexual abuse by their fathers "collude in the incestuous liaison and play an active and even initiating role in establishing the pattern" (Henderson, 1975, as cited in Herman, 1981, p. 40).

By portraying children as sexual beings who both desired and initiated sexual 'activity' with adult men, men's sexual access to them could be conveniently framed as an exercise in children's autonomy, or an expression of their sexuality. Under the guise of children's sexual rights, laws which prevented men's sexual use of children, like age of consent laws, could be condemned on the basis of repressing children's sexuality. For example, sexologist Edwin J. Haeberle called for the abolition of laws against incest on the basis that children were being denied "their right to sexual satisfaction" (see Herman, 1981, p. 25).

The concept of children's right to 'sexual expression' was useful for paedophiles and their supporters, as it allowed them to shift the focus from men's sexual predation to children's 'right' to engage in sexual relations with them. Feminist writer, Florence Rush, pointed out that, "The call for the sexual freedom of children, in the name

of child welfare, is transparently focused upon adult gratification"
(1980, p. 187).

As Sheila Jeffreys put it: "The children, of course, were not
clamouring for sexual liberation – only the men who wanted to use
them" (Jeffreys, in Clásicas y Modernas, 2021).

Second wave feminists exposing child sexual abuse

One of the most significant achievements of second wave feminists
was exposing the phenomenon of incest and child sexual abuse
which they recognised as a male abuse of power. Feminists
debunked the myth of 'stranger danger', bringing to light the
prevalence of fathers and male relatives as perpetrators of abuse,
and citing the unequal power relations between adults and children.

One of these women was Florence Rush, author of *The Best
Kept Secret: Sexual Abuse of Children* (1980). Having spent years
working as a social worker, Rush observed a pattern of child sexual
abuse involving an adult male perpetrator and a female child,
which was widespread across all areas of society. She identified
men's sexual abuse of children as a national epidemic, writing that,
"Sexual abuse of children is not an occasional deviant act, but a
devastating commonplace fact of everyday life" (1980, p. xii).

Rush exposed the ways men's sexual use and abuse of children,
primarily girls, had been historically condoned through religion and
scripture, in Greece's golden age, the Victorian era, child marriage
in India, child prostitution, sexual slavery and child pornography,
through myths, fairy tales, films, advertising and literature, and laws
made by men and in the interest of men.

Feminists like Rush who objected to men's sexual abuse
of children were charged with repressing children's sexuality.
Researcher Steven Angelides (2004) accused feminists of
disempowering children by contributing to the repression of their
sexuality:

> The discourse of child sexual abuse has expanded at the expense
> of a discourse of child sexuality ... The feminist use of power has

functioned to evade, silence, erase, and repress a signifier of child sexuality (p. 142).

Indeed, Angelides alleged feminists' "utter disregard" for child sexuality was "as damaging to a child's social and psychological well-being as the discounting of the reality of sexual abuse" (p. 158).

While feminist objections were characterised as sexual repression, men's sexual abuse of children was portrayed as sexual liberation. Campaigning against laws criminalising paedophilia, founder of NAMBLA (North American Man/Boy Love Association), David Thorstad, wrote:

> We are engaged in a war between the forces of sexual liberation on the one hand and the forces of sexual repression on the other. Man/Boy love and cross generational sex have become the cutting edge of that war. Repeal all age of consent laws!!! Freedom of sexual expression for all!!! (Thorstad, 1979, cited in Rush, 1980, pp. 188–189).

Paedophiles portrayed as victims

Queer theorists and paedophile apologists portrayed paedophiles as an oppressed, stigmatised minority subjected to persecution, hatred and civil rights violations. They framed objections to paedophilia, and laws criminalising child sexual abuse, as an attack on "erotic communities" (Rubin, 1984/2006, p. 145) arguing that age of consent laws which prevented men's sexual access to children, and laws criminalising child pornography, represented the regulation of sexual behaviour, the violation of civil liberties and further victimisation of paedophiles.

Despite paedophiles being almost exclusively adult men, and their victims always children, paedophile defenders have engaged in a staggering reversal of reality, positioning *paedophiles* as the vulnerable group of the two. In *Thinking Sex* (1984/2006), one of the foundational texts of queer theory, Gayle Rubin characterised paedophiles as "the victims of a savage and undeserved witch hunt" (p. 147), casting men who sexually abuse children, and those who desire to do so, as the victims – not the children they abuse, who are made invisible. While male abusers were positioned as the legitimate victims of a conservative moral panic, the children they raped were relegated to the status of 'invented' victims:

> When the furore has passed, some *innocent erotic group has been decimated,* and the state has extended its power into new areas of erotic behaviour. The system of sexual stratification provides *easy victims who lack the power to defend themselves,* and a pre-existing apparatus for controlling their movements and curtailing their freedoms. The stigma against sexual dissidents renders them morally *defenceless* ... Moral panics rarely alleviate any real problem, because they are aimed at chimeras and signifiers. They draw on the pre-existing discursive structure *which invents victims in order to justify treating 'vices' as crimes* (Rubin, 1984/2006, p. 163, italics added).

Queer theorists, too, argued that men's sexual use of children was not inherently abusive or harmful, and that children were not necessarily victims, but often willing participants. In *The Aftermath of the Great Kiddy-Porn Panic of '77,* writer Pat (now Patrick) Califia wrote:

> Any child old enough to decide whether or not she or he wants to eat spinach, play with trucks, or wear shoes is old enough to decide whether or not she or he wants to run around naked in the sun, masturbate, sit in somebody's lap, or engage in sexual activity (Califia, 1994).

The language commonly used to refer to paedophiles functioned to obscure the reality of the power disparity between men and children, and to paint men's sexual abuse of children as a relationship. Men who sexually abused children were euphemistically referred to as "boy lovers," "men who love underage youth" and "those whose eroticism crosses generational boundaries" (Rubin, 1984/2006, p. 145; p. 147; p. 151). Men's sexual abuse of children was white-washed as "cross-generational encounters" (p. 153) or "intergenerational sex" (Angelides, 2004, p. 142), which is certainly more palatable than 'men who rape and sexually abuse children'.

Child pornography 'panic'

Queer theorists and paedophile advocates argued the criminal-isation of child pornography (now known as child sexual abuse material) was primarily an attack on the rights of paedophiles. In the late 1970s in the US, a federal law was introduced which prohibited any depiction of children nude or engaged in sexual activity. In 1990, a Supreme Court ruling criminalised the possession and viewing of child pornography. Naturally, defenders of paedophilia argued the laws against child pornography were unreasonable, preventing "even the private possession" of pornography involving children (Rubin, 1984/2006, p. 146). But as Rubin noted critically, outside of NAMBLA and the American Civil Liberties Union, "no one raised a peep of protest" (p. 146).

Paedophile defenders dismissed and downplayed the serious-ness of child pornography as a crime against children. Califia lamented the "panic" over the "bogeyman" of child pornography or "kiddy-porn" (1991/1994). Califia claimed its prevalence had been exaggerated and that most of the content was not necessarily abusive, being mainly comprised of depictions of naked children and young people engaged in sexual activity with each other. Only a "very tiny proportion" showed adults "engaged in sexual contact with minors" and it would be "a mistake to characterise all child porn as 'a record of abuse'":

> Sometimes it was a record of children's exhibitionism and free erotic play with one another. Sometimes it was a record of adolescent vanity, pride, and budding sexuality. Sometimes it preserved a moment of exceptional trust and pleasure *between partners whose ages would normally have kept them apart* (Califia, 1991/1994, italics added).

The creation and distribution of child pornography was downplayed as nothing more than "boy-lovers" merely taking (pornographic) photos of their "youthful partners," images which they might share with their friends – and "doesn't everyone take pictures of loved ones?" (Califia, 1991/1994).[9]

In *Thinking Sex* (1984/2006), Rubin recounted the case of a photographer, Jacqueline Livingston, who was fired and under threat of prosecution for taking and distributing photographs of her seven-year-old son masturbating. This was shared as evidence of the frightening climate created by the "child porn panic," with Rubin concluding: "It is easy to see someone like Livingston as a victim of the child porn wars. It is harder for most people to sympathise with actual boy-lovers" (p. 147). Paedophiles and their supporters portrayed the adult men as stigmatised victims who risked punishment for producing child pornography – not the children used in its production.

Rise of the paedophile rights movement

Attitudes towards child sexual abuse have evolved considerably since then. It is now widely understood that children cannot consent to sex acts with adults, that sexual contact between adults and children constitutes sexual abuse, and that sexual abuse is demonstrably harmful to children.

Earlier arguments in support of children's supposed rights to engage in sexual 'relationships' with adult men are unlikely to achieve mainstream acceptance today. It is much more difficult for paedophiles and their defenders to convincingly claim men's sexual use of children is an expression of children's sexual autonomy, or that laws against child sexual abuse – filmed or otherwise – constitute an attack on the civil liberties of paedophiles. As a result, their tactics have changed.

There is now a concerted effort by paedophile rights groups to 'destigmatise' paedophilia and disentangle it from child sexual abuse. Paedophiles have rebranded themselves as 'Minor Attracted

---

9   Pat Califia has since updated her position – see *Public Sex: The Culture of Radical Sex* (2000).

Persons' (MAPS). Some describe themselves as non-offending, non-contact or even "virtuous" paedophiles, claiming they do not sexually abuse children (see Virped, 2012).

With the backing of supportive academics and advocates (who are mostly male), paedophiles continue to portray themselves as an oppressed, stigmatised minority. This is now accomplished through the conceptualisation of paedophilia as a sexual or psychiatric disorder – 'not a choice'. These advocates argue paedophilia is a legitimate, unchangeable sexual attraction or orientation that is outside the control of the individual – a condition that a person (a male) is afflicted with. Where feminists understand paedophilia and child sexual abuse as a male abuse of power, advocates paint paedophiles as victims of their circumstances who are deserving of sympathy, compassion and understanding, lamenting the "unfortunate situation in which they find themselves" (Moen and Sterri, 2018, p. 377).

A number of academics and advocates argue that since paedophiles cannot ethically act on their sexual desires to rape and abuse children, they need to have access to sexual outlets that allow them to simulate it. These include 'virtual' child sexual abuse material (artistic or computer-generated depictions of non-existing children, produced without the use of living children) as well as child sex abuse dolls.

Some paedophile advocates go even further, claiming that providing paedophiles with child-like dolls on which to enact their fantasies of raping children could prevent their abuse of children. David Levy, author of *Love and Sex with Robots* (2007) told *The Guardian*, "It would be better for paedophiles to use robots as their sexual outlets than to use human children" (Levy, 2015 as quoted in Wiseman, 2015). Others have suggested that providing paedophiles with child sex abuse dolls could not only prevent their sexual offending against children, but that failing to do so could put children at risk. In his 2017 paper proposing child "sexbots" be made available to paedophiles for "therapeutic" use, philosopher

Marc Behrendt described the potential cost of *not* providing paedophiles with robotic replica children:

> If the end justifies the means ... any kind of therapeutic option should be considered, analysed, scrutinised, weighed and even tried ... can civil society still afford to take the risk of seeing other unfortunate victims, unwittingly hooked to the appalling web of sex offenders? Other souls traumatised for life? Other murdered children? (Behrendt, 2017, p. 97).

Likewise, Canadian psychologist and neuroscientist, James Cantor, asks, "If we surveyed victims of childhood sexual abuse, I wonder how many would say they WISHED their abusers had a sex doll who might have taken their place?" (Cantor, 2019 as quoted in Nicol, 2019).

Where paedophilic men previously portrayed their sexual access to children as being in children's best interests, they now portray their access to child sex abuse dolls as preventative. Defenders of these technologies do not use the rhetoric of men's sexual rights, which is unlikely to be a winning strategy. Instead, they argue that men's access to child sex abuse dolls could protect children from sexual abuse, and purport to be motivated by a concern for their safety and wellbeing. Framing child sex abuse dolls as potentially preventing child sexual abuse is an approach much more likely to garner support, even in the absence of any evidence to support their claims.

Defenders of men's right to virtual child sexual abuse material and child sex abuse dolls accuse feminists who object of being motivated by a "moral purity agenda" rather than out of any meaningful concern for children (Malcolm, 2021b). One of these, Prostasia Foundation, bills itself as a child protection organisation but campaigns *against* laws criminalising child sex abuse dolls and sexualised depictions of children in drawing and cartoons, objects to sex offender registries and funds research into "fantasy sexual outlets" for paedophiles (Slatz, 2021). Unlike other child protection organisations, Prostasia promotes ageplay, BDSM and kink, and "centers its work around safeguarding the civil liberties of adults" (Férdeline, 2020).

Prostasia Foundation's founding executive director, Jeremy Malcolm, accuses feminists who campaign against child sex abuse dolls – referred to by Prostasia Foundation (2021) as "purity campaigners" – of having a secret agenda to police sexual practices they disapprove of ("Everything but straight, cis, missionary sex is deviant in your book") and an unhealthy interest in other people's sex lives ("your obsession with how other people masturbate is honestly invasive and creepy") (Malcolm, 2021c). Malcolm dismisses feminist objections to child sexual abuse material as purely ideological and unscientific – "moral purity is more important to you than possibly preventing abuse" (Malcolm, 2021d). This is in contrast to those, like him, who support the development of child sex abuse dolls for men's sexual use as rational, scientific and on the side of sexual liberation. Unsurprisingly, they are almost entirely, men.

"It's just a sex toy like any other"

> I don't fucking understand why having (or wanting) A DOLL could be illegal. IS JUST A MANNEQUIN! A FUCKING ITEM, A LIFELESS OBJECT. You can do to IT whatever you want as it's NOT ALIVE and you are THE OWNER (paedophile forum participant, n.d.).

One of the arguments made in support of child sex abuse dolls is that they are sex toys like any other. Prostasia Foundation characterises men's use of child sex abuse dolls as "the personal and private use of sex toys" and claims that laws prohibiting them are therefore "unconstitutional, misguided and immoral" (Prostasia Foundation, 2019). James Cantor posted on Twitter, "I'm okay with latex sex toys and I don't care what they look like," and "Australia protecting society from crimes against latex. Thought crimes against latex" (Cantor, 2018a; 2017).

If child sex abuse dolls are conceptualised as merely sex toys like any other, it could theoretically be argued that they do not raise any unique ethical issues. But child sex abuse dolls, like sex dolls and robots more generally, are distinct from traditional sex toys on the basis of their embodiment in human form – most often, the female form. They are not simply latex masturbation aids, they are lifelike, anatomically correct representations of girls with penetrable orifices and marketed for men's sexual use. The childlike appearance is not incidental; it is the very point. Child sex abuse dolls are intentionally designed to look and feel like a real child, to facilitate men's fantasy experience of raping a little girl. If the products were truly nothing more than a latex sex toy, there would be no need for them to be shaped like little girls in the first place.

The ability to simulate child sexual abuse is precisely the drawcard for male users. Indeed, this is why some academics pitch child sex abuse dolls as an alternative to sexually abusing a child, because they believe the dolls could function as surrogates for children. Equating men's use of child sex abuse dolls modelled on the bodies of little girls with the use of a sex toy is a deliberate attempt to decontextualise men enacting their fantasies of child sexual abuse from a wider culture in which men sexually abuse girls at an alarming rate.

"It's a victimless crime – you can't rape a robot"

Defenders of men's access to child sex abuse dolls and robots argue that given they are objects, not moral agents, they cannot be victims of rape or child sexual abuse and conclude there is no harm: you can't rape a robot (Malcolm, 2021a; Prostasia Foundation, 2019b). But feminist objections are not focused on harm to dolls, robots, or inanimate objects – they are concerned with harm to children.

Advocates argue that men's sexual use of child sex abuse dolls is a victimless crime in the same way they have argued men's consumption of virtual child sexual abuse material (virtual child pornography) is a victimless crime, because no child is being abused in its production (Malcolm, 2021e). But legitimising children as appropriate objects of male sexual desire and gratification puts them at risk, normalising men's sexual use and abuse of children and encouraging offenders.

According to the United Nations Report of the Special Rapporteur on the sale and sexual exploitation of children, including child prostitution, child pornography and other child sexual abuse material (2020), sexualised depictions of "non-existing" children serve to normalise men's sexual abuse of children:

> The increased accessibility and availability of child sexual abuse material online appears to normalise this crime and may encourage potential offenders and increase the severity of abuse. This includes new phenomena, such as drawings and virtual representations of non-existing children in a sexualised manner, widely available on the Internet.
>
> The increasing social acceptance of early sexualisation is exacerbated by the widespread dissemination of child sexual abuse material on the Internet and the production of highly realistic representations of non-existing children. This objectification of children comforts offenders in their actions (UN Special Rapporteur, 2020, pp. 11–12).

Similarly, feminist sociologist Gail Dines argued that even where actual children are not used in its production, pornographic content featuring adult women portraying children undermines important social norms that define children as off limits for men's sexual use. Writing on 'Pseudo Child Pornography' (also known as 'Teen' or 'Barely Legal' porn) where women are depicted as children and styled with braces and pigtails, Dines described how the eroticisation of children could influence male consumers' attitudes toward children and put them at risk:

> Once they click on these sites, users are bombarded – through images and words – with an internally consistent ideology that legitimises, condones, and celebrates a sexual desire for children. The norms and values that circulate in society and define adult-child sex as deviant and abusive are wholly absent in PCP

[Pseudo Child Pornography] and in their place a cornucopia of sites that deliver the message (to the viewer's brain, via the penis) that sex with children is hot fun for all ... There is a wealth of research within media studies that shows people construct their notions of reality from the media they consume, and the more consistent and coherent the message, the more people believe it to be true ... This does not mean that all men who masturbate to PCP will rape a child, or even be sexually attracted to a child. What it does mean, however, is that on a cultural level, when we sexualise the female child, we chip away at the norms that define children as off limits to male sexual use (Dines, 2011, pp. 7–8).

"They could prevent child sexual abuse"

Perhaps the most common claim in support of child sex abuse dolls is that they could prevent 'real' child sexual abuse by providing a sexual outlet to men who might otherwise sexually abuse children. This is the claim made by a child sex abuse doll owner in a piece published on Prostasia Foundation's blog, entitled, 'How dolls could help prevent abuse'. The author, who uses a pen name, disputes any link between child sex abuse dolls and child sexual abuse. He claims that child sex abuse doll owners feel a strong desire to nurture, likening the experience to owning a pet dog, but also acknowledges that some doll owners "receive sexual gratification" from their child-like dolls. He accuses lawmakers proposing legislation to criminalise child sex abuse dolls of eliminating outlets for paedophiles, "taking away dolls from those who have few if any other outlets of sexual expression." The potential criminalisation of child sex abuse dolls, he argues, represents an attempt to outlaw "the sexual thoughts and private behaviours" of doll owners. He threatens that preventing men's access to child sex abuse dolls may push them over the edge and result in them abusing a 'real' child (Doll, 2018).

However, a 2019 report from the Australian Institute of Criminology found not only that there is no evidence child sex abuse dolls could prevent sexual abuse, but that they could *increase* the risk of child sexual abuse. Authors Rick Brown and Jane Shelling reviewed the literature on sex dolls, child sexual exploitation material and sexual offending against children. They warned that child sex abuse doll use could lead to an escalation in sexual offences against children, desensitise users to the harm of sexual abuse (as dolls do not offer any emotional feedback), that they could be used to groom children for abuse, and "promote a continuum of behaviour that results in contact offending, by bridging the gap between fantasy and reality" (Brown and Shelling, 2019, p. 4).

Rather than preventing men's sexual abuse of children, using a child sex abuse doll could represent an escalated method of engaging with child sexual abuse material. On a child abuse spectrum from viewing child sexual abuse material to contact offending, performing sex acts on a child sex abuse doll may be understood as a natural progression from viewing child sexual abuse material, and a step closer to sexually abusing a child. As Open University lecturer, Litska Strikwerda, acknowledges, using a child sex robot could be a much closer experience to sexually abusing a child (Strikwerda, 2017, p. 144).

According to Marie-Helen Maras and Lauren Shapiro from City University of New York, recent UK arrests for importing child sex abuse dolls indicate that offenders escalate from viewing child sexual abuse material to engaging in physical acts on child sex abuse dolls. In these cases, viewing child sexual abuse material did "whet the appetite of the perpetrators" as their "thoughts" – fantasies about sex acts against children – became "behaviours" – through purchasing the child sex abuse doll and performing sex acts on it (Maras and Shapiro, 2017, p. 7).

Men's sexual preferences – even their desires to rape children – are elevated to the status of 'needs' that must be met. Underpinning calls to make child sex abuse dolls available to paedophilic men is the acceptance of men's sexual preferences as absolute; the belief they have a right to sex in any way they want it, and that anything less is deprivation. The academics and advocates who support the development of child sex abuse dolls are so deeply committed to their belief in the male sex right that their answer to men who want to sexually abuse children is not to challenge their sexual appetites, not to encourage the pursuit of healthier practices or relationships that do not involve children, but rather to endorse the manufacture of replica children with penetrable orifices so they can enact their rape fantasies unimpeded.

Child sex abuse doll advocates fail to consider the wider cultural context in which men sexually offend against girls – a system of institutionalised male dominance and a culture that eroticises girls.

Girls are routinely presented as sexually available and appealing in media and advertising. Many women report first experiencing sexual attention from adult men as girls (see Moran, 2020). 'Teen porn' is consistently one of Pornhub's most popular search terms. 'Barely Legal' pornography depicting teens with pigtails, flat chests and braces is widely available, even sold in some Australian newsagents and petrol stations. School girls are fetishised, and sexy school girl costumes are sold in mainstream retailers. Australian grassroots campaigning movement 'Collective Shout: for a world free of sexploitation' has exposed major bookstores and online marketplaces like Amazon and Bookworld selling 'erotic' eBooks that feature incest and child sexual abuse. Sexualised images and videos of underage and even pre-pubescent girls can easily be found on social media apps like Instagram, typically met with predatory sexual comments from adult men (Liszewski, 2019).

Men's demand for child sex abuse dolls modelled on the bodies of pre-pubescent girls cannot be separated from a wider culture in which girls are sexualised and treated as objects of men's sexual entertainment. Rather than finding more avenues to accommodate men's sexual desires for girls, a better approach is to address the root of these desires, to challenge the cultural factors at play that encourage and legitimise men's sexual entitlement and predation on girls.

Lack of empirical evidence

There is no reliable empirical data on child sex abuse dolls and their potential impact on child sexual abuse, and it is hard to imagine how this could ethically be carried out.

Craig Harper, advisor to pro-sex doll lobby group Prostasia Foundation, and Rebecca Lievesley authored what they believe to be the "first empirical analysis of child-like sex doll ownership" (Harper and Lievesley, 2022, p. 23). They sourced data from child sex abuse doll owners and 'MAPS' (Minor Attracted Persons) – also known as paedophiles – who did not own a doll, comparing their psychological characteristics and proclivities for sexual aggression.

Harper and Lievesley dismissed research that argued child sex abuse dolls encourage the sexual objectification of children and normalise their abuse as being one-sided. These arguments against child sex abuse dolls, they argue, "[fail] to acknowledge the potential for dolls playing a role in the prevention of child sexual abuse" (p. 4).

The authors rejected the report by the Australian Institute of Criminology which concluded that there was no evidence child sex abuse dolls could prevent child sexual abuse, and that they could increase the risk of abuse. They wrote it was "concerning that a government-supported agency would seek to promote one side of this debate and downplay the validity of the other" (p. 5). As Harper and Lievesley see it, it is "equally plausible" that doll ownership could be associated with an increased risk of sexual offending against children – or they could prevent abuse.

Harper and Lievesley considered three different theoretical models for child sex abuse doll ownership. First, dolls as protective: that child dolls could be protective of sexual aggression by providing a safe outlet for paedophiles. Second, dolls as risk-enhancing: that child-like dolls could increase owners' likelihood of sexually abusing children. Finally, dolls as functional life tools: non-sexual reasons why owners might own dolls. For example, they argue, paedophiles may not have the chance to have children, and owning a child sex abuse doll could provide the "opportunity to mimic these processes in surrogate parental relationships where sexual motivations for ownership may be secondary" (p. 8). In other words, a child sex abuse doll could allow its male owner to experience the fantasy of being a parent, while still being able to use their 'child' for sexual gratification.

Despite finding doll owners engaged in more objectifying behaviours and expressed greater levels of hypothetical enjoyment in abusing a child, Harper and Lievesley found no evidence for the 'Dolls as risk-enhancing' theory, where dolls could increase owners' likelihood of abusing a child, and claimed that concerns child sex abuse doll owners could be at higher risk of sexually offending against children "might be misplaced":

> In contemporary discourse around doll ownership, there is a tendency to frame doll sex ownership through a risk-based lens. Within these discussions there is an implicit (and sometime explicit) assumption that the ownership of sex dolls – particularly dolls that resemble children – is inherently risky and associated with a proclivity for sexual offending. We found no such evidence of this within our data, with the behavioral proclivity and arousal to hypothetically engaging in child sexual abuse being lower among child-like sex doll owners than among MAPs who did not own a sex doll (p. 24).
>
> [Doll owners were] more likely to exhibit schizotypal personality traits, to report engaging in sexually objectifying behaviors than non-owners, and reported more anticipated enjoyment in relation to hypothetical child sexual abuse scenarios. However, they were significantly less sexually preoccupied than non-owners, less antisocial, and demonstrated a lower level of self-reported arousal to child sexual abuse scenarios (pp. 21–22).

However, Harper and Lievesley did not find any evidence that owning a child sex abuse doll could reduce paedophiles' risk of sexually abusing a child.

The authors believe doll owners are "equally using their dolls for sexual reasons, emotional reasons and 'other' reasons," such as for hobbies, non-sexual intimacy and "photography and art" – although, based on paedophile forums where doll owners share pornographic photos and videos of their dolls, "photography and art" frequently means producing their own virtual child sex abuse material (pp. 15–16).

Does it matter if doll owners report using dolls for non-sexual reasons, if they are also using their child-like dolls for sexual gratification? How many of these men would purchase a child-sized doll without penetrable orifices, or purely for "hobbies," if they could not also abuse it sexually?

A limitation of the research as reported by the authors was the self-reporting method of data collection. The validity of self-reported data is always questionable – people are often biased when it comes to reporting their own experiences, and their responses may be influenced by what they believe is socially acceptable.

When paedophiles are being asked to self-report around their own sexual offending against children and their desires to rape and abuse children, it is conceivable that their responses might not be truthful. And, as the authors themselves acknowledged, given the growing number of countries and states criminalising child sex abuse dolls,

> it is still possible that some participants may have responded in such a way to avoid increased perceptions of the risks posed by those who own child-like sex dolls (p. 27).

Regardless, the authors call for further research to explore child sex abuse dolls for use in "therapeutic contexts," and to find sexual outlets for paedophiles. The prevention of child sexual abuse appears to be a secondary consideration:

> In contrast to moralistic publications citing the potential risks of such dolls in relation to child sexual abuse we found evidence for their functional use. In light of this, we hope that those working in psychological and sex science can launch systematic studies

that explore how to best support MAPS in their search for safe sexual outlets, with ultimate aims of improving levels of mental health in this population and, subsequent to this, the prevention of the sexual abuse of children (p. 29).

While advocates portray child sex abuse dolls as possibly being the means of preventing child sexual abuse, by providing men who might otherwise rape and sexually abuse them with a "safe sexual outlet," only 1.2 per cent of doll owners cited preventing offending behaviour as a reason for owning a child-like doll.

Men still sexually offend against children

The most compelling evidence against child sex abuse doll advocates' claims comes from doll owners themselves. For many of these men, it is not as simple as 'choosing' between a doll *or* a child. Despite owning a child sex abuse doll, they still sexually offend against children.

In the UK, seizures of child sex abuse dolls have led investigators to identify previously unknown sexual offenders against children (Rawlinson, 2017). Men who are found in possession of a child sex abuse doll are typically also found in possession of images and videos of child sexual abuse material, featuring the abuse, rape and torture of children. A press release from New York Congressman, Dan Donovan, who introduced the *Curbing Realistic Exploitative Electronic Pedophilic Robots (CREEPER) Act* to ban the importation and distribution of child sex abuse dolls, revealed that of the 128 child-like dolls seized in the UK, 85 per cent of the men who imported them were also found in possession of child sexual abuse material (Stop Abuse Campaign, 2017).

South Australian man, Shane Andrew Lunnay, who livestreamed himself having sex with a child sex abuse doll, was found with images of children being sexually abused, as well as drawings and animated content depicting the sexual abuse of children aged between three and 12 (Bermingham, 2020).

In England, former soldier Richard Turner was found with a child sex abuse doll as well as 100,000 images of child sexual abuse material (203 of these being the most serious kind) and pleaded guilty to ten charges of sexually offending against children (Hetherington, 2019).

In the US, James Randall Adams was found with 62,381 images and 738 videos on his phone which were mainly child sexual abuse material, as well as an adult female-bodied mannequin and a bound child mannequin that both appeared to be used as sex dolls (Reavy, 2021a).

An unnamed Utah man was found with eight child sex abuse dolls, two of them dressed in the gown from Disney's *Frozen*, after a social media company reported him to police for uploading and distributing child sexual abuse material (Reavy, 2021b).

A police raid of the home of New South Wales man, Stephen Capsis, turned up a child sex abuse doll and a 'trove' of child sexual abuse material. Capsis had been caught at the beach filming intimate videos of young girls in bikinis and zooming in on their genitals using a covert device attached to his car (Lockley and Barr, 2021).

There are plenty more news reports like this – and these are just the cases where the offenders were caught. Owning a child sex abuse doll or consuming virtual child sexual abuse material did not prevent these men, nor any of the others in a growing number of reported cases like these, from sexually offending against children.

Dolls made in the likeness of actual children

There is also evidence of male owners of child sex abuse dolls incorporating real children into their doll usage. Police charged Adelaide man, Adam Neil Wonnocott, after they caught him with hundreds of images of child sexual exploitation material. Among them were those where faces of children known to him had been superimposed over the faces of abused children. He also owned five homemade child sex abuse dolls. One of these dolls, dressed in girls' clothing and with a sex toy built into it, had a laminated photo of a real child's face attached to its head (Mott, 2021).

Victorian primary school teacher, James William Treasure, filmed himself having intercourse with a child sex abuse doll in a school uniform with masks made from school photos of his students. Police also found videos of sex acts on which Treasure had digitally imposed his own face and that of one of his young students, as well as thousands of child abuse images and several covert recording devices (Hobday, 2021).

Doll manufacturers have created child sex abuse dolls in the likeness of actual children. In 2020, an American mother named Terri shared her distress upon discovering a child sex abuse doll modelled on her eight-year-old daughter. She had received a Facebook message from a friend alerting her to images of a child sex abuse doll being sold on Amazon. The doll bore a striking resemblance to her daughter Kat. One picture appeared to recreate a photo of her daughter that she had previously shared to Facebook:

> I read the message from my friend and saw the image, and I instantly started to cry uncontrollably. I was completely over-whelmed with a mix of emotions that I've never felt before.
>
> The image of the doll looked very similar to a photo I've taken of my daughter. This image had the same socks as my daughter and the same pose as my daughter on our sofa at home. She had that same sweatshirt and facial features as that image, even the same stuffed animal!

Amazon removed the doll from sale several days after Terri contacted them, but she has since learned the doll was also listed elsewhere (Child Rescue Coalition, 2020).

A Collective Shout investigation spearheaded by Melinda Liszewski exposed child sex abuse doll sellers on Etsy producing child sex abuse dolls modelled off real children. Liszewski posed as a potential customer and approached sellers on the platform. One claimed to have made a particular child doll in the likeness of a 14-year-old Instagram model. Liszewksi then sent through computer-generated images of non-existing children and asked if the seller could make dolls that resembled the girls in the photos, to which the seller agreed (Hall, 2020).

But it's not just Etsy sellers offering child sex abuse dolls made in the likeness of actual children. A number of doll manufacturers offer customisation. While it's not uncommon for buyers to design their own child doll by selecting hair and eye colour, body type and a range of other features, some manufacturers will also produce child sex abuse dolls based on a photo.

Catdoll, a child sex abuse doll manufacturer which makes dolls as small as 102 cm, is one such retailer:

> Catdoll can accept customized order. We can make the doll as your picture. Any questions pls contact us! [sic].

In a discussion thread about child sex abuse dolls on a popular paedophile forum, one user shared his enjoyment of a child sex abuse doll he owned that bore a striking resemblance to a child in his life:

> One of my girls closely, and I mean CREEPILY closely, resembles someone I fixated on. As if fixation isn't creepy enough. But this is someone I fantasized about daily, ejaculated to daily, and escalated with. Escalated. 'Yes, I'll play Twister with you and your brother'. Someone I knew. But I had a doll that creepily resembled her. Have. Still do. What normalized my relationship with that little girl, what made it all possible, was that doll. I was able to be her 'uncle' because that darker stuff was sublimated in a piece of plastic. I may have cum buckets into and onto that doll, but I never once paid that little girl inappropriate attention ... As my relationship with that doll deepened, I 'naturally' bought clothes that my object of fixation might wear, things I saw her wear, to heighten the effect.

While the man believed owning a child sex abuse doll in the likeness of a girl he wanted to sexually abuse prevented him abusing her, the girl has already been victimised and violated.

As this example illustrates, child sex abuse dolls do not just aid in the fantasy of abusing a generic, hypothetical child; they allow users to victimise a specific child without even having physical access to her.

Far from being a 'victimless' crime, the development of child sex abuse dolls facilitates a new form of technologically-mediated sexual abuse, one where men can simulate the rape, abuse and torture of specific children using dolls made in their likeness.

Where to from here?

The child sex abuse doll market is still in its infancy, yet children have already been harmed through their manufacture and use. Experts predict that child sex abuse robots will be next, and may already be in development. Australian Border Force has reported a 653 per cent increase in detections of child sex abuse dolls over the last two years (Chung, 2021). As the technology advances, more children will be put at risk of serious harm.

We need state parties around the world to act urgently to uphold the rights of children –society's most vulnerable members, through uniform legislation criminalising the manufacture, sale, importation and possession of child sex abuse dolls. There must be significant penalties associated with these offences to reflect cultural values that children – whether in real life or depicted as sex abuse dolls – are off limits for men's sexual use. Australia's laws could serve as a useful model for other countries and states considering their options.

Global online marketplaces which have hosted child sex abuse doll listings need to implement strong policies and practices that prevent the sale of these products on their platforms, permanently banning sellers in breach of terms and conditions, and passing their details to law enforcement for further investigation. They need to incur penalties if they don't take action.

Men's sexual entitlement to the bodies of children must be challenged, not accommodated. This should not have to be said. Rather than attempting to cater to men's sexual desires for children through the development of sexual outlets made in their likeness, we need to question and critique men's desires, to challenge the male sex right, and address a wider patriarchal culture that endorses and facilitates these developments.

Crimes of rape and child sexual abuse are not prevented with men practising on child sex abuse dolls. Normalising men's sexual use and abuse of children might benefit some men, but it will never be in the best interests of children.

Resistance

The future

If we do nothing, what will the future look like for women and girls? Realistic lifelike sex dolls and robots are still in their infancy today – what will the impacts be on all of us in another ten or 20 years?

The growing acceptance of sex dolls as replica women puts all women at risk. It further entrenches men's sexual entitlement and women's status as subordinate objects, which will likely contribute to increased degradation and violence towards women.

As silicone replica women become more normalised and mainstream, more men could view dolls as a legitimate alternative to a relationship with a woman – even a preferable option – and develop increasingly hostile and objectifying views towards women. Or, having sexually trained and practiced on dolls, enter into relationships with women believing they too should be submissive and obedient, and tolerate any and all of their sexual fetishes without complaint.

Given the interactive nature of sex robots, technological advances could intensify the potential harms to women and girls. Future developments in sex robot technology could result in increasingly realistic female-bodied robots – robots that can walk, talk and more convincingly play the role of female partner. Where a sex doll is a lifeless replica woman that never says no, a sex robot could be a responsive replica woman that always says yes.

Complete with a customised, programmed personality and with any 'undesirable' personality traits weeded out, a sex robot could give the appearance of reciprocation, performing enthusiasm and enjoyment for sex acts that would be considered painful, humiliating and degrading by many women. It could encourage its male user through words and moans and beg for more. How might this type of sexual encounter shape men's beliefs and expectations around sexual relations with women and how they should play out? And what might be the impacts of this for women?

Sex robots could both facilitate and encourage men's practice of violence against women and girls. They could be programmed to respond favourably to sexualised abuse and torture – providing positive reinforcement – or to actively resist and cry, depending on customer preference.

Just as some sex doll owners have practised perpetrating sexual violence, BDSM and torture on their dolls, interactive sex robots could further allow predatory men to practise and finetune their 'skills'. Where one doll owner shared his progress in tying up his doll, rendering it 'completely helpless' and unable to move, a sex robot could provide the opportunity to rehearse more complicated scenarios. What if she [sic] fights back? What if she [sic] runs? With a sex robot, a predatory man could prepare for all of these possibilities and more.

A few women and girls have already suffered the indignity of having sex dolls made in their image. What will be the impact on women and girls when interactive sex robots are mainstream and can be modelled on their bodies, voices and mannerisms? How might such products be utilised for harassment, abuse and 'revenge porn'?

More women will feel pressured to tolerate their partner's sex doll use as normal and acceptable. Not only will they feel powerless to do anything about it, they will believe that *they* are the problem;

that they must be prudish, that they are not hot enough, and that they are failing to meet their husband's sexual demands. Women will be subjected to humiliation, heartbreak and trauma, pressured into submitting to unwanted, violent and degrading sex knowing he will turn to his doll if she says no. Women will never be able to live up to men's fantasy of the perfect, compliant fuck doll, and may be irreparably damaged in their attempts to do so.

Some advocates argue sex dolls and robots could function as therapeutic tools. If they are indeed legitimised as such, men could be emboldened to carry their 'companion' dolls around with them like their guide dogs. Just as with South Korea after the legalisation of life-size dolls, there will likely be a proliferation of sex doll venues, like 'sex doll experience' cafes and brothels. Men could impose their sex dolls and robots on women and children in the public space, with women having no recourse because the products are deemed 'therapeutic'.

If sex dolls are sanctioned for 'therapeutic use', men who own them could portray themselves as a stigmatised minority in need of legal protections. Just as there have been calls for paedophilia to be added to the LGBT+ umbrella (see Cantor, 2018b; Harper, 2019), doll owners and advocates could lobby for their place in the ever-growing acronym. Sex doll owners could become a legally protected class, with feminist objections framed as intolerance, bigotry and hate speech.

Sex dolls and robots in the female form function as an endorsement of men's sexual rights, with women and girls positioned as sexual objects. The production of these products further cements women's second-class status.

Global resistance

Women are mobilising in response to the development of female-bodied sex dolls and robots. From activists to academics and around the globe, women and male allies are speaking out.

Campaign Against Porn Robots (UK)

The Campaign Against Porn Robots (formerly the Campaign Against Sex Robots) was launched in 2015 by anthropologist Professor Kathleen Richardson to oppose the development of sex robots in the female form. Campaign goals include abolishing 'pornbots' in the form of women and girls, and to offer an "alternative, relational model of sex and sexuality informed by mutuality."[10]

Collective Shout (Australia)

One of the major players in the fight against the global trade in child sex abuse dolls is Australian grassroots campaigning movement Collective Shout: for a world free of sexploitation.[11] Collective Shout challenges the objectification of women and sexualisation of girls in media, advertising and popular culture, targeting corporates which exploit the bodies of women and girls to sell products and services and campaigning to change their behaviour.

Collective Shout has taken on a number of online platforms facilitating the sale of child sex abuse dolls.

National Center on Sexual Exploitation (US)

The National Center on Sexual Exploitation (NCOSE), a leading US-based non-profit organisation that links all forms of sexual exploitation, has also challenged platforms hosting the sale of sex dolls in the form of women and children.[12]

The Feminist Academy of Technology and Ethics –
FATES (international)

The Feminist Academy of Technology and Ethics was founded in 2021 by a group of women in academia around the world as a much-needed feminist response to technologies that harm women

---

10 <www.campaignagainstsexrobots.org>.
11 <www.collectiveshout.org>.
12 <www.endsexualexploitation.org>.

and girls. Members of 'The Fates' have spent more than a year engaging with feminist literature and developing theory around sex dolls and robots.[13]

Campaigns against sex doll sellers

Amazon
Every year, NCOSE launches their 'Dirty Dozen' list – naming 12 mainstream corporations that facilitate sexual exploitation and abuse. In 2016, the group named global online marketplace Amazon for selling sex dolls, some of which were child-like.

NCOSE raised awareness through social media posts and press statements, and mobilised supporters through petitions and email campaigns, where they would email Amazon customer service and executives, calling for the products to be removed. They persisted for several years.

In 2018, Amazon finally removed most child sex abuse dolls, though they still pop up occasionally. The following year, the group exposed a child sex abuse doll being sold on Amazon – a young looking doll with a flat chest that was pictured gagged and tied up with rope. After media picked up the story, the listing was quickly removed.

Now Amazon has a policy prohibiting products that depict child abuse and exploitation, but as Haley Halverson, NCOSE Vice President and Director of the International Centre on Sexual Exploitation, points out: "Policies on paper aren't always the same as policies in action." But there appears to have been a significant change from when they first exposed sex dolls on Amazon from 2018 onwards, and the company has largely removed full-bodied sex dolls from sale.

Many online platforms are not effectively enforcing their policies against child abuse material, but as Halverson points out

---

13   See forthcoming publication, Kathleen Richardson and Charlotta Odlind (eds), *Man-made women: The sexual politics of sex dolls and robots.*

this is a matter of priority. "We're not seeing cocaine being sold on Amazon, or videos of child sex abuse – so there is some control," she says.

Wish

In 2018, Collective Shout discovered child sex abuse dolls being sold on major budget shopping app Wish. The dolls, which were designed to look like pre-teen girls, were typically between 100 and 130 cm tall, with emphasis on their 'flat chests'. They were deliberately posed and styled to accentuate their youthful appearance and to convey a sense of innocence, photographed as though they were shyly looking away from the camera, with their heads tilted in a childlike way. The images conveyed vulnerability, with dolls posed sitting crossed-legged on a bed, wearing nothing but knickers, or naked in the bath. Along with the appearance of innocence and vulnerability, there was a suggestion of sexuality. Childlike dolls were photographed with singlet straps falling off shoulders, fingers lingering over their mouths, or shorts pulled down to expose their private parts.

In addition to child sex abuse dolls, Collective Shout found replica child body parts – disembodied child heads, legs and feet – all marketed for men's sexual use.

Product descriptions of the dolls emphasised how 'real' they feel:

> Buying a sex doll can be a daunting task at first, but understanding the various types and benefits of each will make your decision easier. Sex dolls are made with natural, safe, real silicone so that each gorgeous girl feels real.

Even sex dolls with large, porn-style, out of proportion breasts appeared to be very child-like. One of these wore a cropped Pikachu t-shirt, from the cartoon Pokemon. It is likely these dolls were intended for men's paedophilic use, with large breasts added to get around customs.

After Collective Shout exposed Wish on their Facebook page, the company responded in a comment on the post indicating they were not aware of how such items had "made it onto their platform" and were committed to removing them when they find them. But months went by and the products remained, and Wish ignored further correspondence from the campaign group.

Wish is not a small company. It is reportedly worth US$8.5 billion and boasts 300 million subscribers around the world. If executives had any real desire to rid their platform of child sex abuse dolls, they had the means to do it.

Collective Shout's next move was to share the content found on Wish on social media, posting damning listings of child sex abuse dolls and how they were being marketed to Twitter, tagging sponsors and shareholders. They found and contacted a major seed funder who shared their disgust, and promised to let the Wish board know that this was not how he envisioned his investment being spent.

Within days, Collective Shout received a message from Wish CEO Peter Szulczewski advising that child sex abuse dolls were being removed from the site. From beginning to end, the campaign took four months. But, like on other online platforms, child sex abuse dolls continue to pop up from time to time.

Alibaba

In 2020, the Collective Shout team became aware of child sex abuse dolls being sold through the Alibaba Group, a Chinese conglomerate of e-commerce platforms including Alibaba.com (its business-to-business arm) and Aliexpress.com (its business to consumer arm). The dolls were modelled on the bodies of prepubescent girls, toddlers and babies, tagged with search terms like 'young girl', 'flat chest', and 'sex dolls for men'. Some were just 65 cm tall, roughly the size of a six-month-old infant. One of the sellers shared a video of an anatomically correct baby sex doll, demonstrating how it could be used.

Collective Shout asked how, when there was more awareness of child sexual abuse and its harms than ever before, a multi-billion-dollar mainstream corporation like Alibaba could profit from normalising the rape of babies.

After attracting international media attention for their campaign, and within a week, Alibaba issued a statement saying they had removed child sex abuse dolls from their platform.

Members of the Collective Shout team continued to work with Alibaba, and as a result of ongoing positive communications, the company announced in November 2021 that they were geo-blocking the sale of all sex dolls to Australia and issued the following statement:

> Alibaba and AliExpress have voluntarily removed the sale of all sex dolls to users in Australia. We appreciate the support of Collective Shout and the broader community as part of the ongoing battle against the exploitation of women and children (Collective Shout, 2020).

Etsy

That same year, Collective Shout exposed global online marketplace Etsy selling hundreds of lifelike sex dolls, many of which were designed and sized to look like children. Shortly after, they uncovered a range of incest and child abuse-themed merchandise as well, complete with slogans like 'Daddy's little cock whore', 'Harder Daddy' and 'Daddy's cum dumpster'.

Upon discovering these products on the platform, Etsy seller Anna Cordell – also a fashion designer, musician and mother of five – shut down her Etsy store in response. Backed by Collective Shout, Anna created a change.org petition calling on Etsy to stop selling incest and child-abuse themed merchandise:

> I couldn't believe what I was seeing! Child sex abuse dolls and body parts, child abuse and incest-themed products with slogans begging a father to use his own daughter. Not just words but images depicting young girls as wanting to be violated.

So I've launched this petition because I don't think child sexual abuse should be normalised and turned into something to make money from (Cordell, 2021).

After being exposed for selling illegal child sexual abuse material, child sex abuse doll sellers on Etsy updated their product descriptions in an apparent attempt to avoid scrutiny.

Collective Shout campaigner Lyn Kennedy observed a distinct change in the language used in product descriptions for child sex abuse dolls and replica child body parts. Where previously, these products were promoted with search terms like 'flat chest', 'loli', 'mini', and 'young girl', after Collective Shout's campaign revealed Etsy sellers trading in illegal child sexual abuse material, many of these product descriptions were updated with the terms 'adult' and 'full size'.

While Etsy sellers edited damning product descriptions that made clear their dolls were modelled on the bodies of girls, they did not remove the actual products. The only changes made were to the promotional material:

One listing on Etsy (documented November 2021) featured images of a child-size doll (available for purchase in a range of heights including 100 cm and 140 cm), with facial features unequivocally modelled off a young girl. Product descriptors included 'adult', 'D cup', 'woman' and 'girlfriend' (Kennedy, 2021).

Kennedy documented a number of doll listings with dolls clearly made in the likeness of girls but listed as 'adult' dolls. Some were pictured with children's paraphernalia, like Hello Kitty underwear. One listing for an 'Adult sex doll petite size' offered a choice of 21 different heads, many of which appeared to be modelled on prepubescent girls. In the product description for one child sex abuse doll, the term 'dwarf' was used. Another doll was marketed as a 'lady' despite being 140 cm, the height of an average nine-year-old child.

A childlike replica mouth marketed as a male masturbator had been sold as 'Custom Asian Girl Handmade', but after Collective Shout called out Etsy for hosting racialized child sexual abuse material that fetishised Asian girls, the seller removed the term 'girl' from the listing. The childlike mouth remained.

Despite significant, negative media attention in mainstream Australian news outlets (see Hall, 2020; Cross, 2022) for facilitating the sale of illegal child sex abuse dolls, an increasing number of Etsy sellers shutting up shop in response, and Anna's petition attracting more than 65,000 signatures to date, Etsy has still failed to respond. But the campaign is not slowing down, and Etsy has made NCOSE's 2022 Dirty Dozen list.

Where to from here?

In the midst of an epidemic of violence against women, where men's violence remains one of the greatest threats to women's health, wellbeing and lives, sex dolls and robots are the absolute last thing women need. We need men to recognise women's humanity, not to further endorse the view that women are objects, or are interchangeable with objects, or mere tools for men's sexual relief.

As Andrea Dworkin said of prostitution, "I want to bring us back to basics" (Dworkin, 1993). I would like to do the same here. What we are talking about is the production of silicone replica women and girls, for men's unlimited sexual use. To look at it in a slightly different way, these are dolls overwhelmingly made in the likeness of one half of the population, to be sexually used by the other half.

Female-bodied sex dolls and robots are an expression of woman-hating. We only need to look at the news to see how pervasive misogyny is in our culture – we cannot afford for things to get even worse. We need to expose, confront and challenge male sexual entitlement, the belief that men have a right to sex and that they are entitled to women's bodies. We need to call out and fight the everyday sexual objectification of women, not legitimise and reinforce it through the development of sex dolls and robots. We need to resist.

As a culture, we need to decide what we value, and where our priorities truly lie. Do we endorse men's complete freedom to enact any and all of their porn-fuelled sexual desires on compliant replica women? Or are we committed to upholding the human rights of women and girls? It cannot be both.

We can't do it halfway. We cannot advocate for women's human rights and simultaneously endorse their objectification and dehumanisation. We cannot oppose male violence against women while tolerating men's sexual entitlement. Either we believe in the rights, dignity and humanity of women, or we do not.

So do we?

References

Allen, Felix. (2017). My sex doll is so much better than my real wife. *New York Post*, 30 June. <https://nypost.com/2017/06/30/i-love-my-sex-doll-because-she-never-grumbles/>

Anderson, Dan. (2018). 4 reasons why you should consider gifting a sex doll to your husband. *Sex Doll Genie*, 30 June. <https://sexdollgenie.com/blogs/news/4-reasons-why-you-should-consider-gifting-a-sex-doll-to-your-husband>

Andreallo, Fiona. (2019). Robots with benefits: how sexbots are marketed as companions. *The Conversation*, 14 November. <https://theconversation.com/robots-with-benefits-how-sexbots-are-marketed-as-companions-126262>

Angelides, Steven. (2004). Feminism, child sexual abuse, and the erasure of child sexuality. *GlQ: A Journal of Lesbian and Gay Studies*, 10(2), pp. 141–177.

Appel, Jacob M. (2010). Sex rights for the disabled? *Journal of Medical Ethics*, 36(3), pp. 152–54.

BBC. (22 March 2018). Sex doll 'brothel': Xdolls escapes Paris council censure. <https://www.bbc.com/news/world-europe-43506621>

BBC Three. (2018). The Future of Sex? Sex Robots And Us. [online video]. <https://www.youtube.com/watch?v=kGTI2_O9v_Y>

Bardhan, Ashley. (2022). Men Are Creating AI Girlfriends and Then Verbally Abusing Them. *Futurism*, 18 January. <https://futurism.com/chatbot-abuse?fbclid=IwAR3NXag6c6x_Sa2BbMiffl06KjZr1Pqbkvn YvpfFw572bpmoKpkWpAC5D-M>

Behrendt, Marc. (2017). Reflections on Moral Challenges Posed by a Therapeutic Childlike Sexbot. In *Love and Sex with Robots*. Singapore: Springer, pp. 96–113.

Bell, Jess. (2020). I fell in love with a robot. *7News*, 25 December. <https://7news.com.au/lifestyle/relationships/i-fell-in-love-with-a-robot-c-1710777>

Bell, Richard. (2021). Life-like sex dolls business owner Jade Stanley horrified by demands for child-like models. *Entertainment Daily*, 1 February. <https://www.entertainmentdaily.co.uk/tv/life-like-sex-dolls-maker-jade-stanley-horrified-by-child-like-model-requests/>

Bender, Lauretta and Abram Blau. (1937). The Reaction of Children to Sexual Relations with Adults. *American Journal of Orthopsychiatry 7*, p. 514.

Bermingham, Kathryn. (2020). Shane Andrew Lunnay, who streamed himself having sex with a child-like sex doll, jailed for importing child exploitation material. *News.com.au*, 23 September. <https://www.news.com.au/national/south-australia/shane-andrew-lunnay-who-streamed-himself-having-sex-with-a-childlike-sex-doll-jailed-for-importing-child-exploitation-material/news-story/77b2497ad47f68c7bf1ce342525c4ea6>

Best, Shivali. (2020). Sex robot firm teams up with FBI following surge in requests for 'childlike bots'. *Mirror*, 10 September. <https://www.mirror.co.uk/tech/sex-robot-firm-teams-up-22658584>

Bindel, Julie. (2018). Why fully decriminalising prostitution hurts all women. *Australian Summit Against Sexual Exploitation*, 15 August. <https://www.youtube.com/watch?v=LSTHZdXr0dk>

Blackall, Molly. (2021). 'Stop the Breast Pest': MP's 'horror' at being photographed while breastfeeding. *The Guardian*, 2 May. <https://www.theguardian.com/lifeandstyle/2021/may/01/labour-mp-stella-creasy-horror-photographed-while-breastfeeding-prompts-campaign>

Bordoll. (2017). Bordoll: the new generation of sex. <www.bordoll.de>

Boseley, Matilda. (2020). Revenge porn in Australia: The law is only as effective as the law enforcement. *The Guardian*, 9 May. <https://www.theguardian.com/society/2020/may/09/revenge-porn-in-australia-the-law-is-only-as-effective-as-the-law-enforcement>

Brown, Rick and Jane Shelling. (2019). Exploring the implications of child sex dolls. Trends and Issues in Crime and Criminal Justice. *Australian Institute of Criminology*, No. 570.

Califia, Pat. (1991). Feminism, Pedophilia, and Children's Rights. In *Paidika*, Vol. 2, No. 4, reprinted in *The Culture of Radical Sex* (1994). <https://www.ipce.info/ipceweb/Library/califa_feminism.htm>

Califia, Pat. (1994). The Aftermath of the Great Kiddy-Porn Panic of '77'. *The Culture of Radical Sex*. <https://www.ipce.info/ipceweb/Library/califa_aoc_frame.htm>

Cantor, James. (2017). 5 February. <https://twitter.com/JamesCantorPhD/status/828009118736777216>

Cantor, James. (2018a). 13 October. <https://twitter.com/JamesCantorPhD/status/1050816822189154304>

Cantor, James. (2018b). 9 December. <https://twitter.com/jamescantorphd/status/1071499969910198274>

Child Rescue Coalition. (2020). A Mother's Story: Daughter's Photo Stolen and Likeness Turned Into A Child Sex Doll. *Child Rescue Coalition*, 1 October. <https://childrescuecoalition.org/educations/child-sex-doll>

Chung, Laura. (2021). Man charged over alleged importation of childlike sex dolls. *The Age*, 10 September. <https://www.theage.com.au/national/nsw/man-charged-over-alleged-importation-of-childlike-sex-dolls-20210907-p58pjv.html>

Clásicas y Modernas. (2021). Pensar el Feminismo 15 mañana. <https://www.youtube.com/watch?v=5Ejz59OKQ04>

coco Qin. (2017). Emma the humanoid sex robot from AI Tech. <https://www.youtube.com/watch?v=X94wrX0Oo-U>

Cohen Aris, Yael. (2019). 29 July. <https://www.instagram.com/p/B0eOu36BJXI/?hl=en>

Collective Shout. (22 July 2020). Collective Shout welcomes Alibaba's removal of child sex abuse doll listings. <https://www.collectiveshout.org/alibaba_removes_dolls>

Combatting Child Sexual Exploitation Legislation Amendment Bill 2019. (2019). Exploratory Memorandum. <https://parlinfo.aph.gov.au/parlInfo/download/legislation/ems/r6376_ems_0921e440-c545-4239-b247-57193a7710e5/upload_pdf/713291.pdf;fileType=application%2Fpdf#search=%22legislation/ems/r6376_ems_0921e440-c545-4239-b247-57193a7710e5%22>

Cordell, Anna. (2021). Etsy: Stop selling incest and child abuse themed merch! *Change.org*. <https://www.change.org/p/etsy-stop-selling-incest-and-child-abuse-themed-merch>

Cottle, Robin. (2020). 'Terrifying' custom sex doll created to look like singer leaves her 'physically sick'. *Daily Star*, 14 December. <https://www.dailystar.co.uk/news/latest-news/terrifying-custom-sex-doll-created-23164892>

Coyle, Haley. (2018). Sex doll 'slaughter': Mutilated and decapitated figure found dumped in bushes. *Daily Star*, 25 March. <https://www.dailystar.co.uk/news/latest-news/sex-doll-murder-thailand-jack-16856432>

Cross, Julie. (2022). Etsy accused of profiting from child sex abuse material on its site. *Daily Telegraph*, 4 March. <https://www.dailytelegraph.com.au/news/etsy-accused-of-profiting-from-child-sex-abuse-material-on-its-site/news-story/c9648cea8c57f3efa6e6dad7af5a2d50?btr=13c4d0907def95846c0bb67ed06404be>

Croucher, Shane. (2018). Robot Rights: California Cult Leader Starts Crowdfunding Campaign for 'Consent-focused Robot Brothel'. *Newsweek*, 8 November. <https://www.newsweek.com/robot-rights-california-cult-leader-starts-crowdfunding-campaign-consent-1206986>

Cybrothel. (2021). Cybrothel. <https://cybrothel.com/de/dolls>

Danaher, John. (2015). Building Better Sex Robots: Lessons from Feminist Pornography. In Y. Zhou and M. Fischer (eds). *AI Love You: Developments on Human-Robot Intimate Relations*. Singapore: Springer.

Danaher, John. (2017). The Symbolic-Consequences Argument in the Sex Robot Debate. In John Danaher and Neil McArthur (eds). *Robot Sex: Social and Ethical Implications*. Cambridge, MA: MIT Press.

Danaher, John, Brian D. Earp and Anders Sandberg. (2017). Should we campaign against sex robots? In John Danaher and Neil McArthur (eds). *Robot Sex: Social and Ethical Implications*. Cambridge, MA: MIT Press.

Davis, Allison. (2018). Are we ready for robot sex? *New York Magazine*, 14 May. <https://www.thecut.com/2018/05/sex-robots-realbotix.html>

Delicado-Moratalla, Lydia. (Forthcoming). Mapping the uses of 'sex' dolls: pornographic content, doll brothels and similarities with rape. In Kathleen Richardson and Charlotta Odlind (eds). *Man-made Women: The Sexual Politics of Sex Dolls and Sex Robots*. Social and cultural studies of robots and AI series. London: Palgrave-Macmillan.

Devlin, Kate. (2015). In defence of sex machines: why trying to ban sex robots is wrong. *The Conversation*, 17 September. <https://theconversation.com/in-defence-of- sex-machines-why-trying-to-ban-sex-robots-is-wrong-47641>

Devlin, Kate. (2018). *Turned On: Science, Sex and Robots*. London: Bloomsbury Publishing.

Di Nucci, Ezio. (2011). Sexual rights and disability. *Journal of Medical Ethics*, 37(3), pp. 158-161.

Di Nucci, Ezio. (2017). Sexual Rights, Disability and Sex Robots. In John Danaher and Neil McArthur (eds). *Robot Sex: Social and Ethical Implications*, Cambridge, MA: MIT Press.

Dines, Gail. (2010). *Pornland*. North Melbourne: Spinifex Press.

Dines, Gail. (2011). The New Lolita: Pornography and the Sexualization of Childhood. In Abigail Bray and Melinda Tankard Reist (eds). *Big Porn Inc: Exposing the Harms of the Global Pornography Industry*. North Melbourne: Spinifex Press.

DollBanger. (29 December 2021). My (unsolicited) advice for those interested in creating doll content Part 1. <https://dollbangerblog.com/blog/my-unsolicited-advice-for-those-interested-in-creating-doll-content-part-1/>

Doll, Lexie. (2018). How dolls could help prevent child sexual abuse. *Prostasia Foundation*, 15 November. <https://prostasia.org/blog/dolls-prevent-child-sexual-abuse/>

Doll Orphanage. (2022). Protection Services. <https://webshop.lolidolls.nl/protection-services/>

Doll Podium. (2022a). Makena – Jungle Queen 162cm. <https://dollpodium.com/collections/black/products/makena>

Doll Podium. (2022b). Shanice – Love Physique 162cm. <https://dollpodium.com/collections/black/products/shanice-killer-physique>

Doll Wives. (2021). Should you buy your husband a sex doll? <https://dollwives.com/should-you-buy-your-husband-a-sex-doll/>

Döring, Nicola and Sandra Pöschl. (2018). Sex toys, sex dolls, sex robots: Our under-researched bed-fellows. *Sexologies*, Vol. 27, No. 3, pp. 51–55.

DS Doll Robotics. (2021). Approaching Sex Robotics. <https://dsdollrobotics.com/approaching-sex-robotics/>

Dubé, Simon and Dave Anctil. (2020). Sex in space: Could technology meet astronauts' intimate needs? *The Conversation*, 20 February. <https://theconversation.com/sex-in-space-could-technology-meet-astronauts-intimate-needs-131630>

Dworkin, Andrea. (1981). *Pornography: Men Possessing Women*. New York: Plume.

Dworkin, Andrea. (n.d.) [online video]. https://www.youtube.com/watch?v=iLWgGdFEC-8

Dworkin, Andrea. (1993). Prostitution and Male Supremacy. *Michigan Journal of Gender and Law*, Vol. 1, No. 1, pp. 1–12.

Earp, Brian D. and Ole Martin Moen. (2016). Paying for sex—only for people with disabilities? *Journal of Medical Ethics*, 42(1), pp. 54–56.

elledoll. (13 November 2021). When The Wife Is Pregnant, Buy A Sex Doll For Your Husband. <https://elledoll.com/when-the-wife-is-pregnant-buy-a-sex-doll-for-your-husband/>

Ekberg, G 2004, 'The Swedish law that prohibits the purchase of sexual services: Best practices for prevention of prostitution and trafficking in human beings', *Violence against women*, Vol. 10, No. 10, pp.1187–1218.

Ekman, Kajsa Ekis. (2013). *Being and Being Bought: Prostitution, Surrogacy and the Split Self.* North Melbourne: Spinifex Press.

Farley, Melissa, Emily Schuckman, Jacqueline M. Golding, Kristen Houser, Laura Jarrett, Peter Qualliotine and Michele Decker. (2011). Comparing Sex Buyers with Men Who Don't Buy Sex: 'You can have a good time with the servitude' vs 'You're supporting a system of degradation'. *Psychologists for Social Responsibility Annual Conference, Boston.*

Férdeline, Ayden. (2020). Facts About Prostasia. <https://www.prostasia.info/>

Field, Emma. (2020). Mallacoota College investigated after 'totally unacceptable' sex doll incident on muck-up day. *ABC News*, 20 November. <https://www.abc.net.au/news/2020-11-20/mallacoota-college-sex-doll-muck-up-day-tim-cashmore/12902108>

Fong, Mei. (2017). Sex Dolls Are Replacing China's Missing Women. *Foreign Policy*, 28 September. <https://foreignpolicy.com/2017/09/28/sex-dolls-are-replacing-chinas-missing-women-demographics/>

Frymorgen, Tomasz. (2017). Sex robot sent for repairs after being molested at tech fair. *BBC*, 29 September. <https://www.bbc.co.uk/bbcthree/article/610ec648-b348-423a-bd3c-04dc701b2985>

Giard, Agnès. (2018). Duplicates of minors sold as 'Love Dolls': Disturbance in sexual representation. *Hybrid*, Revue des arts et médiations humaines, (04).

Griffin, Susan. (1981). *Pornography and Silence: Culture's Revenge against Nature.* New York: Harper and Row.

Gutiu, Sinziana. (2012). Sex Robots and Roboticization of Consent. *We Robot Conference*, Coral Gables, Florida.

Gutiu, Sinziana. (2016). Sex robots and roboticization of consent. In Ryan Calo, A. Michael Froomkin and Ian Kerr (eds). *Robot Law*. Cheltenham, UK: Edward Elgar Publishing.

Häggström, Simon. (2016). *Shadow's Law: The True Story of a Swedish Detective Inspector Fighting Prostitution.* Los Angeles: SCB Distributors.

Hall, James. (2020). Etsy seller providing childlike sex dolls modelled off 14-year-old Instagram star. *News.com.au*, 9 December. <https://www.

news.com.au/technology/online/etsy-seller-providing-childlike-sex-dolls-modelled-off-14yearold-instagram-star/news-story/5baac0a4b8c02dd3dd711d57e1bd9531>

Harper, Craig. (2019). [Twitter] 23 December. <https://twitter.com/CraigHarper19/status/1175865745789607936>

Harper, Craig. A. and Rebecca Lievesley. (Forthcoming). Exploring the ownership of child-like sex dolls.

Harper, Craig. A., Rebecca Lievesley and Katie Wanless. (Forthcoming). Exploring the psychological characteristics and risk-related cognitions of individuals who own sex dolls. *Journal of Sex Research.*

Héloïse. (2022) [Twitter] 19 March. <https://twitter.com/belivetsgloves/status/1504982067091845123>

Henderson, D. James. (1975). Incest. In Alfred M. Freedman, Harold I. Kaplan and Benjamin J. Sadock (eds). *Comprehensive Textbook of Psychiatry.* Baltimore: The Williams & Wilkins Company, 2nd ed.

Herman, Judith. (1981). *Father Daughter Incest.* Cambridge MA: Harvard University Press.

Hess, Amanda. (2011). What is 'feminist porn'? Your sex and gender morning roundup. *ABC 7 News*, 2 May. <https://wjla.com/archive/what-is-feminist-porn-your-sex-and-gender-morning-roundup-10584>

Hetherington, Graeme. (2019). Former soldier found with child-like sex doll jailed for sex crimes. *The Northern Echo*, 13 August. <https://www.thenorthernecho.co.uk/news/17832017.former-soldier-found-child-like-sex-doll-jailed-sex-crimes/>

Hobday, Liz. (2021). Paedophile primary teacher uses school photos of his students to make sick videos of himself with a childlike sex doll dressed in uniform. *Daily Mail*, 8 November. <https://www.dailymail.co.uk/news/article-10176409/James-William-Treasure-Paedophile-primary-teacher-dresses-sex-doll-school-uniform.html>

Hunter, Rose. (2022). *Body Shell Girl: A Memoir.* Mission Beach: Spinifex Press.

I LOVE MISSDOLL. (2019). [Twitter] 8 February. <https://twitter.com/loveMISSDOLL/status/1093588889858498560>

Illes, Judy and Farhad R. Udwadia. (2019). Sex robots increase the potential for gender-based violence. *The Conversation*, <https://theconversation.com/sex-robots-increase-the-potential-for-gender-based-violence-122361>

Indiegogo. (2018). Eve's Robot Dreams. <https://www.indiegogo.com/projects/eve-s-robot-dreams#/>

James, John. (1970). *The Facts of Sex*. Princeton, NJ: Vertex.

Jecker, Nancy S. (2021). Nothing to be ashamed of: sex robots for older adults with disabilities. *Journal of Medical Ethics*, 47(1), pp. 26–32.

Jeffreys, Sheila. (2008). Disability and the male sex right. *Women's Studies International Forum*, Vol. 31, No. 5, pp. 327–335.

Jeffreys, Sheila. (2020). *Trigger Warning: My Lesbian Feminist Life*. Mission Beach: Spinifex Press.

Jeffreys, Sheila. (2022). *Penile Imperialism. The Male Sex Right and Women's Subordination*. Mission Beach: Spinifex Press.

Kasulis, Kelly. (2019). South Korea's sex doll industry stirs controversy with 'life-size' imports. *The World*, 20 April. <https://theworld.org/stories/2019-08-19/south-koreas-sex-doll-industry-stirs-controversy-life-size-imports>

Kennedy, Lyn. (2021). 'Adult', 'full size', detachable breasts: How child sex abuse doll sellers evade detection. *Collective Shout*, 13 December. <https://www.collectiveshout.org/how_sex_abuse_doll_sellers_evade_detection>

Kennedy, Lyn. (2022). Pink-cladding: The corporates who use women to cover their sexploitative tracks. *Collective Shout*, 21 January. <https://www.collectiveshout.org/pink_cladding_corporates_use_women_to_cover_tracks>

Kleeman, Jenny. (2020). *Sex Robots and Vegan Meat: Adventures at the Frontier of Birth, Food, Sex & Death*. New York: Pegasus Books.

Klein, Renate. (2017). *Surrogacy: A Human Rights Violation*. Mission Beach: Spinifex Press.

Klein, Wilhelm E.J. and Vivian Wenli Lin. (2018). 'Sex robots' revisited: a reply to the campaign against sex robots. *ACM SIGCAS Computers and Society*, Vol. 47, No. 4, pp. 107–121.

Korea Times. (2021). Supreme Court bans imports of childlike sex dolls. *Korea Times*, 28 January. <https://www.koreatimes.co.kr/www/nation/2021/11/251_319446.html?tw>

Kristof, Nicholas. (2020). The Children of Pornhub. *New York Times*, 4 December. <https://www.nytimes.com/2020/12/04/opinion/sunday/pornhub-rape-trafficking.html>

Langton, Rae. (2009). *Sexual Solipsism: Philosophical Essays on Pornography and Objectification*. Oxford: Oxford University Press.

Levy, David. (2007a). *Love and Sex with Robots: The Evolution of Human-Robot Relationships*. New York: Harper.

Levy, David. (2007b). Robot prostitutes as alternatives to human sex workers. In *IEEE International Conference on Robotics and Automation*, Rome, Vol. 14.

Liszewski, Melinda. (2019). A day of the girl on Instagram: posed, exposed and at risk. *Collective Shout*, 10 October. <https://www.collectiveshout.org/a_day_of_the_girl_on_instagram_posed_exposed_and_at_risk>

Locatelli, Chloe. (2018). 'The Perfect Companion': From Cyborgs to Gynoids-Sex Robots and the Commodification of Authentic Intimate Experience. Masters Thesis. Universidad de Granada.

Lockley, Mike. (2019). Businesswoman calls for £5k sex dolls to be made available for free on the NHS. *Birmingham Mail*, 16 November. <https://www.birminghammail.co.uk/news/midlands-news/businesswoman-sex-dolls-available-nhs-17256873>

Lockley, Kate and Eliza Barr. (2021). Steven Capsis charged with fresh possession of child porn offences. *Daily Telegraph*, 5 May. <https://www.dailytelegraph.com.au/newslocal/stgeorge-shire-standard/steven-capsis-charged-with-fresh-possession-of-child-porn-offences/news-story/122eb092b908ecde1f21bc68ed21fb87?btr=4732472f5181977811ea4c5412fe0d74>

MacKinnon, Catharine. (1989). *Toward A Feminist Theory of State*. Cambridge, MA: Harvard University Press.

MacKinnon, Catharine. (1993). *Only Words*. Cambridge, MA: Harvard University Press.

MacWilliam, Shirley. (Forthcoming). Playthings and Corpses – Turning Women into Dead Body Objects: Sexual Objectification, Victimisation, Representation and Consent in Art and Sex Dolls/Robots. In Kathleen Richardson and Charlotta Odlind (eds). *Man-made Women: The Sexual Politics of Sex Dolls and Sex Robots*. Social and cultural studies of robots and AI series. London: Palgrave-Macmillan.

Maeda, Toshi. (2007). Japan's lonely hearts turn to dolls for sex, company. *Reuters*, July 18. <https://www.reuters.com/article/us-japan-sex-dolls-idUKSP10422420070718>

Malcolm, Jeremy. (2021a). [Twitter] 18 June. <https://twitter.com/qirtaiba/status/1405715180277813248>

Malcolm, Jeremy. (2021b). [Twitter] 24 June. <https://twitter.com/qirtaiba/status/1407865086664794114>

Malcolm, Jeremy. (2021c). [Twitter] 24 June. <https://twitter.com/qirtaiba/status/1407754968782688256>

Malcolm, Jeremy. (2021d). [Twitter] 24 June. <https://twitter.com/qirtaiba/status/1407851020919603204>

Malcolm, Jeremy. (2021e). [Twitter] 5 November. <https://twitter.com/qirtaiba/status/1456649544700088320>

Mallows, Melissa. (Forthcoming). Modern-Day Pygmalions – Reproducing the Patriarchy. In Kathleen Richardson and Charlotta Odlind (eds). *Manmade Women: The Sexual Politics of Sex Dolls and Sex Robots*. Social and cultural studies of robots and AI series. London: Palgrave-Macmillan.

Maras, Marie Helen and Lauren Shapiro. (2017). Child sex dolls and robots: more than just an uncanny valley. *Journal of Internet Law*, 21(5), pp. 3–21.

McArthur, Neil. (2017). The Case for Sexbots. In John Danaher and Neil McArthur (eds). *Robot Sex: Social and Ethical Implications*. Cambridge, MA: MIT Press.

McCurry, Justin. (2020). South Korea football league imposes record fine on FC Seoul over sex dolls outrage. *The Guardian*, 21 May. <https://www.theguardian.com/world/2020/may/21/south-korea-football-league-imposes-record-fine-on-fc-seoul-over-sex-dolls-outrage>

McDonnell-Parry, Amanda. (2018). Can Sex Robots Give Consent? *Rolling Stone*, 26 November. <https://www.rollingstone.com/culture/culture-news/sex-doll-robots-consent-760101/>

McInerny, Liam. (2022). Bodybuilder obsessed with sex dolls says 'it's like necrophilia' but cops can't stop him. *Daily Star*, 7 January. <https://www.dailystar.co.uk/news/weird-news/bodybuilder-obsessed-sex-dolls-says-25881268>

McKeganey, Neil and Marina Barnard. (1996). *Sex Work on the Streets: Prostitutes and Their Clients*. Buckingham: Open University Press.

McVey, Laura, Lauren Gurrieri and Meagan Tyler. (2020). The structural oppression of women by markets: the continuum of sexual violence and the online pornography market. *Journal of Marketing Management*. <DOI: 10.1080/0267257X.2020.1798714>

Mencken, Walter. (2020). Newly reopened restaurants prepare to enforce social distancing with surplus sex dolls. *San Diego Reader*, 29 May. <https://www.sandiegoreader.com/news/2020/may/29/newly-reopened-restaurants-prepare-enforce-social-/>

Michael, Tom. (2016). Sex robots modelled on your favourite celebs set to take over the market, expert warns. *News.com.au*, 5 December. <https://www.news.com.au/technology/gadgets/sex-robots-modelled-on-your-favourite-celebs-set-to-take-over-the-market-expert-warns/news-story/c6d3b0754933a20f22851e663b822f3b>

Migotti, Mark and Nicole Wyatt. (2017). On the Very Idea of Sex with Robots. In John Danaher and Neil McArthur (eds). *Robot Sex: Social and Ethical Implications*. Cambridge, MA: MIT Press.

Misocz, Gunther. (2021). [Twitter] 20 December. <https://twitter.com/heinzsight2020/status/1472785952527433728>

Moen, Ole Martin and Askel Braanen Sterri. (2018). Pedophilia and Computer-Generated Child Pornography. In D. Boonin (ed). *The Palgrave Handbook of Philosophy and Public Policy*. London: Palgrave Macmillan.

Moll, Albert. (1921). *The Sexual Life of the Child*. New York: Macmillan.

Moran, Rachel. (2013). *Paid For: My Journey through Prostitution*. North Melbourne: Spinifex Press.

Moran, Rachel. (2014). Why Jim the johns Article Made My Skin Crawl. *The Prostitution Experience*, 9 August. <https://theprostitutionexperience.com/?p=215>

Moran, Rachel. (2020). [Twitter] 3 April. https://twitter.com/RachelRMoran/status/1245842180507340801

Morin, Roc. (2016). Can Child Dolls Keep Pedophiles from Offending? *The Atlantic*, 11 January. <https://www.theatlantic.com/health/archive/2016/01/can-child-dolls-keep-pedophiles-from-offending/423324/>

Mott, Mitch. (2021). Adam Neil Wonnocott jailed for three years and six months for possessing thousands of child exploitation images. *The Advertiser*, 28 May. <https://www.adelaidenow.com.au/truecrime australia/police-courts-sa/adam-neil-wonnocott-jailed-for-three-years-and-six-months-for-possessing-thousands-of-child-exploitation-images/news-story/ff4c0edf00d713b82e27900979243700?btr=462db2dc176853e063a4db352c0805a6>

Nana (2018). Man divorces wife after 'tasting' sex doll. *Ghana Guardian*. <https://ghanaguardian.com/man-divorces-wife-after-tasting-sex-doll>

Naughty Harbor. (2020a). Nick. <http://siliconeprague.com/nick/>

Naughty Harbor. (2020b). Home. <http://siliconeprague.com/>

Nicol, Ryan. (2019). Governor signs bill outlawing child-like sex dolls. *Florida Politics*, 23 May. <https://floridapolitics.com/archives/297216-governor-signs-bill-sex-dolls/>

Oppenheim, Maya. (2022). Woman reveals 'nightmare' of being 'gang raped' in virtual reality. *Independent*, 3 February. <https://www.independent.co.uk/news/uk/home-news/metaverse-gang-rape-virtual-world-b2005959.html>

ParlVu. (2021). Meeting No. 20 ETHI – Standing Committee on Access to Information, Privacy and Ethics. *ParlVu*, 19 February. <https://parlvu.

parl.gc.ca/Harmony/en/PowerBrowser/PowerBrowserV2/20210219/-1/34789?Language=English&Stream=Video&fbclid=IwAR0FpTn5k1_-497UjnLL_-2kGY4aG2eF45j4dfftEq9HD6_tJjHs2pineKA>

Peeters, Anco and Pim Haselager. (2021). Designing Virtuous Sex Robots. *International Journal of Social Robotics*, 13(1), pp. 55–66.

Pemberton, Becky. (2017). Sex doll more popular than real prostitutes at this brothel. *New York Post*, 22 August. <https://nypost.com/2017/08/22/sex-dolls-are-more-popular-than-real-prostitutes-at-this-brothel/>

Pettinger, Lynne. (2011). 'Knows how to please a man': studying customers to understand service work. *The Sociological Review*, Vol. 59, No. 2, pp. 223–241.

Pettit, Harry. (2021). Sex robots will make humans 'better lovers' by letting us 'explore our wildest fantasies', expert claims. *The Sun*, 21 July. <https://www.thesun.co.uk/news/15649471/sex-robots-humans-better-lovers-explore-wildest-fantasies/>

Playmate Dolls. (2017). Welcome to Playmate Dolls. <https://www.playmatedolls.com/>

Plumridge, Elizabeth W., S. Jane Chetwynd, Anna Reed and Sandra J. Gifford. (1997). Discourses of emotionality in commercial sex: The missing client voice. *Feminism & Psychology*, 7(2), pp. 165–181. <https://doi.org/10.1177/0959353597072002>

Prostasia Foundation. (2019). Our campaigns against doll bans. <https://prostasia.org/sex-doll-laws/>

Prostasia Foundation. (2021a). [Twitter] 16 February. <https://twitter.com/ProstasiaInc/status/1361514207242383360>

Prostasia Foundation. (2021b). [Twitter] 16 February. <https://twitter.com/ProstasiaInc/status/1361514207242383360>

Prostasia Foundation. (n.d.). Exploring the use of fictional and fantasy sexual outlets. <https://prostasia.org/project/research-fund/>

Ramey, James W. (May 1979). Dealing with the Last Taboo. *SIECUS Report*, Vol. VII, No. 5.

Ramaswamy, Chitra. (2022). Photographing breastfeeding mothers? It's the mark of a truly misogynistic society. *The Guardian*, 7 January. <https://www.theguardian.com/commentisfree/2022/jan/07/photographing-breastfeeding-mothers-misogynistic-society-law-voyeurs>

Rawlinson, Kevin. (2017). Child sex doll imports expose previously unknown offenders. *The Guardian*, 31 July. <https://amp.theguardian.com/society/2017/jul/31/child-sex-doll-imports-expose-previously-

unknown-offenders?CMP=share_btn_tw&__twitter_impression
=true>

RealDoll. (2018). Wicked RealDoll. *RealDoll*. <https://www.realdoll.com/
wicked-realdoll/>

RealDoll. (2020). Insert Facilitator Torso. *RealDoll*. <https://www.realdoll.
com/product/insert-facilitator-torso/>

Real Sex Dolls Reviews. (2018). Should I Buy My Husband A Sex Doll?
Real Sex Dolls Reviews, 7 November. <https://realsexdollsreviews.
com/2018/11/07/buy-husband-sex-doll/>

Real Sex Dolls Reviews. (2019). Top 10 Most Popular Sex Doll Brothels.
Real Sex Dolls Reviews, 8 February. <https://realsexdollsreviews.
com/2019/02/08/top-10-popular-sex-doll-brothels/>

Reavy, Pat. (2021a). Orem man charged in child porn case after police
report a disturbing find. *KSL.com*, 17 May. <https://www.ksl.com/
article/50108546/orem-man-charged-in-child-porn-case-after-police-
report-a-disturbing-find>

Reavy, Pat. (2021b). Disturbing find made during child porn investigation.
KSL.com, 8 September. <https://www.ksl.com/article/50237290/
disturbing-find-made-during-child-porn-investigation>

Reed, Jim. (2014). Mega-brothels: Has Germany become 'bordello of
Europe'? *BBC*, 21 February. <https://www.bbc.com/news/world-
europe-26261221>

Reisman, Judith and Mary McAlister. (2018). Deconstructing Dignity by
Eradicating Shame: The Pernicious Heritage of Alfred Kinsey. *Faculty
Publications and Presentations*. 4. <https://digitalcommons.liberty.edu/
psych_fac_pubs/4>

Richardson, Kathleen. (2015). The asymmetrical 'relationship': Parallels
between prostitution and the development of sex robots. *ACM SIGCAS
Computers and Society*, Vol. 45, No. 3, pp. 290–293.

Rivers, David. (2019). Sex robot demand soars for Whitney Cummings
dolls after Netflix hit. *Daily Star*, 3 August. <https://www.dailystar.co.uk/
news/latest-news/sex-robots-whitney-cummings-netflix-18852770>

Roberts, Sophie. (2019). Sex doll customers 'are ordering models that look
like their mates' girlfriends'. *Mirror*, 24 August. <https://www.mirror.
co.uk/news/uk-news/sex-doll-customers-are-ordering-18996096>

Roper, Caitlin. (2021). Pornhub executives stand before Canadian
Parliament over rape and child abuse videos. *Collective Shout*, 23 February.
<https://www.collectiveshout.org/pornhub_executives_stand_before_
canadian_parliament>

Roper, Caitlin. (2022). Etsy selling "black sex slave" dolls for men's sexual use. *Collective Shout*, 6 April. <https://www.collectiveshout.org/etsy_selling_black_sex_slave_dolls>

Rosewarne, Lauren. (2009). Sex on the Street: Outdoor Advertising and the Sexual Harassment of Women. In Melinda Tankard Reist (ed). *Getting Real: Challenging the Sexualisation of Girls*. North Melbourne: Spinifex Press.

Rubin, Gayle. (1984/2006). Thinking Sex: Notes for a Radical Theory of the Politics of Sexuality. In Richard Parker and Peter Aggleton (eds). *Culture, Society & Sexuality*. London: Taylor & Francis Limited.

Rush, Florence. (1980). *The Best Kept Secret: Sexual Abuse of Children*. New Jersey: Prentice-Hall.

Sanders, Teela, Maggie O'Neill and Jane Pitcher. (2009). *Prostitution: Sex Work, Policy and Politics*. London: Sage.

Sex Doll Genie. (2022). AMIRAH – 160CM | 5' 2" – L CUP. <https://sexdoll genie.com/collections/african/products/sex-doll-genie-amirah160l>

Silicon Wives. (2022). Zara: Big Ass Black Sex Doll. <https://www.siliconwives.com/products/zara-black-sex-doll-160cm>

Sinclair, Amy. (2021). Reddit user tells: 'My new flatmate is a sex doll'. *7News*, 7 February. <https://7news.com.au/lifestyle/reddit-user-tells-my-new-flatmate-is-a-sex-doll-c-2101846>

Slatz, Anna. (2021). Exclusive: Dutch Pedophile Selling 'Therapeutic' Baby Sex Dolls. *4W*, 29 November. <https://4w.pub/baby-sex-dolls-pedophile-merchant/>

Stoltenberg, John. (1989/2000). *Refusing to Be a Man: Essays on Sex and Justice*. London: UCL Press.

Stop Abuse Campaign. (2017). Donovan Introduces 'Creeper Act' To Ban Child Sex Dolls. *Stop Abuse Campaign*, 14 December. <https://stopabusecampaign.org/2017/12/14/donovan-introduces-creeper-act-to-ban-child-sex-dolls/>

Story, Rae. (2016). It's in the ignorance: Paying for sex. Blog post in *Permanent Opposition*, 30 March. <https://inpermanentopposition.wordpress.com/2016/03/30/its-in-the-ignorance-paying-for-sex/>

Strikwerda, Litska. (2017). Legal and Moral Implications of Child Sex Robots. In John Danaher and Neil McArthur (eds). *Robot Sex: Social and Ethical Implications*. Cambridge, MA: MIT Press.

Sullivan, Mary Lucille. (2007). *Making Sex Work: A Failed Experiment with Legalised Prostitution*. North Melbourne: Spinifex Press.

Tangermann, Victor. (2021). Police Shut Down China's First Sex Doll Brothel. *Futurism*, 25 March. <https://futurism.com/the-byte/police-shut-down-chinas-first-sex-doll-brothel>

Tankard Reist, Melinda (ed). (2022). *"He Chose Porn Over me": Women Harmed by Men who Use Porn*. Mission Beach: Spinifex Press.

Taunton, Calvin. (2021). I treat the dolls like real people because it's ethical and important. *DollBanger.com*, 28 March. <https://dollbangerblog.com/blog/i-treat-the-dolls-like-real-people-because-its-ethical-and-important/>

The Hook Up Podcast. (2020). Bonus: Cody Heller on sex dolls and feminism. *Australian Broadcasting Corporation*, 29 October. <https://www.abc.net.au/radio/programs/the-hook-up-podcast/cody-heller-on-dan-harmons-sex-doll/12828784>

This Morning. (2017). Holly and Phillip Meet Samantha the Sex Robot [online video]. <https://www.youtube.com/watch?v=AqokkXoa7uE>

Trew, James. (2020). A Sex Doll Stole My Identity. *Playboy*, 7 April. <https://www.playboy.com/read/sex-doll-stole-identity>

Truly. (2021). I Help My Parents Run A Sex Doll Business | My Extraordinary Family. [online video]. <https://www.youtube.com/watch?v=TEuVRRrJOyM>

Uloversdoll. (2022). Lifelike Black Ebony Sex Dolls for Sale Cheapest in Uloversdoll. <https://www.uloversdoll.com/black-sex-dolls.html>

UN Special Rapporteur. (2020). Report of the Special Rapporteur on the sale and sexual exploitation of children, including child prostitution, child pornography and other child sexual abuse material. *Human Rights Council Forty Third Session*, No. 40, 24 February – 20 March. <https://undocs.org/en/A/HRC/43/40>

UNODC. (2018). *Global Study on Homicide 2018*. Vienna.

Unicole Unicron. (2018). Intro to Sex Robots (Robot Series Part 1). [online video]. <https://www.youtube.com/watch?v=pz7k2FO7r0k>

Vadas, Melinda. (2005). The Manufacture-for-use of Pornography and Women's Inequality. *Journal of Political Philosophy*, Vol. 13, No. 2, pp. 174–193.

Valverde, Sarah H. (2012). The modern sex doll-owner: A descriptive analysis. Masters Theses.

Vincent. (2019). A letter to a married woman: Can I allow my husband to have a sex doll? *Sex Doll Marts*, 19 April. <https://www.sexdollmarts.com/blog/a-letter-to-a-married-woman-can-i-allow-my-husband-to-have-a-sex-doll-b0021.html>

Virped. (2012). Welcome to Virtuous Pedophiles. *Virped.* <www.virped. org>

Vue, Toby. (2021). Alleged childlike sex doll shown to jury in ACT trial of Jeffrey Deacon accused of importing prohibited goods. *Canberra Times,* 16 November. <https://www.canberratimes.com.au/story/7512082/ preoccupation-with-young-dolls-led-to-childlike-sex-doll-import-prosecutor/>

Ward, L. Monique. (2016). Media and sexualization: State of empirical research, 1995–2015. *The Journal of Sex Research,* 53(4–5), pp. 560–577.

Whisnant, Rebecca. (2016). 'But what about feminist porn?' Examining the work of Tristan Taormino. *Sexualization, Media, & Society,* Vol. 2, No. 2, pp. 1–12.

Winter, Chase. (2018). Inside Bordoll, a German sex-doll brothel in Dortmund. *DW,* 29 April. <https://www.dw.com/en/inside-bordoll-a-german-sex-doll-brothel-in-dortmund/a-43584520>

Wiseman, Eva. (2015). Sex, love and robots: is this the end of intimacy? *The Guardian,* 13 December. <https://www.theguardian.com/ technology/2015/dec/13/sex-love-and-robots-the-end-of-intimacy>

With All Due Offense. (2018). Women Are In Trouble 2018 Lmao. [online video]. <https://www.youtube.com/watch?v=FLEkEFaZd0c>

Wolski, Gillian. (2020). Bodybuilder weds sex doll after two-year relationship. *Yahoo Lifestyle,* 1 December. <https://au.lifestyle. yahoo.com/bodybuilder-kazakhstan-weds-sex-doll-after-two-year-relationship-235645665.html>

WTHR. (2020). 'Quiet couples' dine at tables to meet social distancing measures. *WTHR,* 14 May. <https://www.wthr.com/article/features/ trending-today/quiet-couples-dine-tables-meet-social-distancing-measures/531-856c5aa6-61bb-4f3b-84b2-c9888b19c903>

Yonhap News Agency. (2021). Sex doll experience cafe condemned by residents in Yongin. *Yonhap News Agency,* 13 April. <https://m-en.yna. co.kr/view/AEN20210413008100315>

Index

Other books from Spinifex Press

"He Chose Porn over Me": Women Harmed by Men Who Use Porn
Melinda Tankard Reist (Ed)

Shattering the popular myth that porn is harmless, the personal accounts of 25 brave women in *He Chose Porn over Me* reveal the real-life trauma experienced by women at the hands of their porn-consuming partners – men who were supposed to care for them.

The women in this book were collateral damage in their partner's insatiable greed for porn. Their stories tell of the crushing of intimacy, respect, connection, love. Porn colonised their families, leaving women rejected and scarred. They were subjected to sexual terrorism in their own homes. The men, turbo-charged by pornography, were intoxicated by sexualised power. They didn't care if they lost everything including their partners.

In this haunting exposé, pornography is rightfully situated as an insidious tool of violence against women. The contributors, now working to re-build their lives, found a confidante in Melinda Tankard Reist who supported them in the sharing of their experiences in these pages, and to warn other women – *don't date men who use porn* …

Occasionally a book comes along that changes the way we think about the world. *"He Chose Porn Over Me": Women Harmed by Men Who Use Porn* is such a book.
  —Gail Dines PhD, Professor Emerita of Sociology.
  President: Culture Reframed

ISBN 9781925950588
ebook available

Penile Imperialism:
The Male Sex Right and Women's Subordination
Sheila Jeffreys

In this blisteringly persuasive and piercingly intelligent book, Sheila Jeffreys argues that women live under penile imperialism, a regime in which men are assumed to have a 'sex right' of access to the bodies of women and girls.

She reasons that the 'sexual revolution' that began in the 1960s unleashed an explicit male sexual liberation and that even now, under current laws and cultural mores, women do not have the right to self-determination in relation to their bodies.

Sheila Jeffreys argues that the exercise of the male sex right has mainstreamed misogynist attitudes and so-called sexual freedom has meant the freedom of men to use women and children with impunity.

Sheila Jeffreys has written a sobering, devastating – indeed, an exceptionally lucid book about male sexual violence and the consequent erasure of womankind.
—Phyllis Chesler, PhD, author of *Women and Madness*,
   A Politically Incorrect Feminist and *Requiem for a Female*
   Serial Killer

In three simple words Sheila Jeffreys exposes the truth behind the havoc wreaked in the lives of women and children in every generation: 'men's sex right'.
—Betty McLellan, PhD, feminist therapist and author of
   Beyond Psychoppression: A Feminist Alternative Therapy

ISBN 9781925950700
ebook available

Big Porn Inc:
Exposing the Harms of the Global Porn Industry
Abigail Bray and Melinda Tankard Reist (Eds)

It is now widely acknowledged that the unprecedented main-streaming of the global pornography industry is transforming the sexual politics of intimate and public life, popularising new forms of hardcore misogyny, and strongly contributing to the sexualisation of children. Yet challenges to the pornography industry continue to be dismissed as uncool, anti-sex and moral panics.

With contributions from leading world experts and activists, Big Porn Inc offers a cutting edge exposé of the hidden realities of a multi-billion dollar global industry that promotes itself as a fashionable life-style choice.

Unmasking the lies behind the selling of porn as 'just a bit of fun' Big Porn Inc reveals the shocking truths of an industry that trades in violence, crime and degradation. This fearless book will change the way you think about pornography forever.

If you care about social justice, buy this book. Big Porn Inc is a must read for anyone interested in the human rights of women and children.
—Christine Stark, author of Nickles and co-editor of Not For Sale

Woman or man, ignore this book at your peril. A remarkable inter-national collection of insightful essays on the growing, poisonous role Big Porn plays in global culture, economics, mores, and violence against women and children. Brava to Spinifex Press for publishing this gift to thoughtful readers.
—Robin Morgan, Author and Activist

ISBN 9781876756895
ebook available

Prostitution Narratives:
Stories of Survival in the Sex Trade
Caroline Norma and Melinda Tankard Reist (Eds)

For too long the global sex industry and its vested interests have dominated the prostitution debate repeating the same old line that sex work is just like any job. In large sections of the media, academia, public policy, Government and the law, the sex industry has had its way. Little is said of the damage, violation, suffering, and torment of prostitution on the body and the mind, nor of the deaths, suicides and murders that are routine in the sex industry.

Prostitution Narratives: Stories of Survival in the Sex Trade refutes the lies and debunks the myths spread by the industry through the lived experiences of women who have survived prostitution. These disturbing stories give voice to formerly prostituted women who explain why they entered the sex trade. They bravely and courageously recount their intimate experiences of harm and humiliation at the hands of sex buyers, pimps and traffickers and reveal their escape and emergence as survivors.

Whatever your stand on prostitution, it's the first-hand stories of women that have to be listened to first. These accounts are among the most unsettling you will ever read, dispelling in just a few pages the comforting fairytales our society has built around 'sex work'.
—Steve Biddulph, author of *Raising Boys*

Compiled by feminists Caroline Norma and Melinda Tankard Reist, the curtain is yanked back and what it reveals is not a pretty sight. Exploitation, trafficking, violence, degradation, depression, drug and alcohol addiction, suicide and murder are part of the territory – not to mention the misogynistic and sadistic nature of the "punters".
—Judith Baragwanath, *North & South Magazine*

ISBN 9781742199863
ebook available

Getting Real:
Challenging the Sexualisation of Girls
Melinda Tankard Reist (Ed)

Girls are portrayed as sexual at younger ages, pressured to conform to a 'thin, hot, sexy' norm. Clothing, music, magazines, toys and games send girls the message that they are merely the sum of their body parts. The effects of prematurely sexualising girls are borne out in their bodies and minds, with a rise in self-destructive behaviours such as eating disorders and self-harm, along with anxiety, depression and low self-esteem.

... the diversity of contributors offers a valuable range of personal and professional insights into an urgent issue and the book will be of great interest to concerned parents and interested readers alike.
—Jo Case, *Bookseller & Publisher*

It's a confronting read, but I think a necessary one to counter-balance the prevalent powers of commercialism.
—Erica Bartle, *Girl with a Satchel blog*

ISBN 9781876756758
ebook available

If you would like to know more about
Spinifex Press, write to us for a free catalogue, visit our
website or email us for further information
on how to subscribe to our monthly newsletter.

Spinifex Press
PO Box 105
Mission Beach QLD 4852
Australia

www.spinifexpress.com.au
women@spinifexpress.com.au